Reader's Digest

The Tools
of War 1939/45
and a chronology of important events

© 1969 The Reader's Digest Association (Canada) Ltd.
215 Redfern Avenue, Montreal, Quebec H3Z 2V9

The credits that appear on page 96 are herewith
made a part of this copyright page.

Published and printed in Canada.

ISBN 0-88850-148-X

Fourth Printing, October 1986

Introduction

The war will be won by science thought-fully applied to operational requirements.

So wrote Air Chief Marshal Sir Hugh Dowding in 1940 after the Battle of Britain—a battle won not only by the pilots of Dowding's Fighter Command but also by the small group of scientists and technicians who developed the RAF's vital radar network and ground-to-air radio control system.

The war fought by the backroom boys was perhaps the most decisive of all. This technological struggle began long before the shooting started, went largely unpublicized and was waged almost invariably against time. It became a war within a war—a never-ending contest to invent and improve the weapons that fighting men needed for victory. The arms, equipment and devices produced from that struggle are *The Tools of War: 1939-45.*

However, this book is not intended to present a complete armory of World War II. Its sole aim is to show a cross-section of the most important arms and equipment used by Canadian servicemen and their German adversaries in the campaigns and actions of that six-year conflict. An illustrated chronology of the war's important events—happenings that changed our world forever—concludes this volume.

The illustrations are grouped in navy, army and air force sections and introduced by articles outlining the seesaw struggles to gain supremacy at sea, on land and in the air. The performance figures and other data are quoted from official manuals and military journals and should be regarded as a guide only. Some figures relate to ideal conditions, and conditions in war were seldom ideal. Equipment, armament and crews carried by ships, aircraft and fighting vehicles varied from one theater of war to another and depended on tactical requirements, the supply situation and numerous other factors.

Although this volume has been written in non-technical language as much as possible, it could not have been prepared without the technical advice of numerous experts, to whom the editors express their gratitude. Special thanks are due to many members of the staff of the Department of National Defense, for their painstaking research and general guidance; to Rear Adm. C. J. Dillon, RCN (ret.), for his collaboration and advice in writing the text and for help in gathering research material for the illustrations; to Mr. E. C. Russell, formerly official historian of the Royal Canadian Navy, and to Wing Comdr. Ralph Manning, DFC, RCAF (ret.), assistant curator of the Canadian War Museum, and other members of the museum staff.

Contents

The War at Sea

The Atlantic was the Allies' lifeline in World War II. Unless they controlled it, they could not maintain their advance base in Britain or launch an invasion of Germany's Fortress Europe. Both sides recognized this strategic situation and, as a result, fought the longest sustained sea battle of modern times—the six-year Battle of the Atlantic. The Royal Canadian Navy was in it from beginning to end, and there it came of age.

From the outset, under plans laid well before the war, Allied merchant ships were organized in convoys, disciplined groups of ships traveling together, and the Germans at first had no effective means of attacking them. In September 1939 Germany had some 60 submarines, half of them small coastal U-boats used for training. Of those capable of high-seas service,

only a portion were available at any one time. Battleships and heavily armed raiders disguised as cargo ships attacked lone merchantmen or stragglers from convoys. Seldom did they attack a whole convoy as the German pocket battleship *Admiral Scheer* did one day in November 1940. The *Scheer* sank only one ship that day—for one single, magnificent reason: the British armed merchant cruiser *Jervis Bay,* hopelessly outgunned, sacrificed herself to let the convoy escape.

Apart from a blockade of Britain by mines and aircraft, the first real German attempt to combat the convoy system came mainly through submarine attacks in coastal areas and the approaches to British ports.

To prepare for larger things, both sides stepped up the production of ships. The Allies built more merchantmen and con-

voy escort vessels, notably at first the corvette; the Germans turned out more and more submarines. As the U-boats increased in number and endurance, they were sent ever farther into the Atlantic, seeking the incoming convoys. They were spurred westward by the growing strength of air and sea patrols in British waters. Soon U-boats were stalking their prey off Newfoundland and Nova Scotia.

At first a convoy had anti-submarine escorts only for a few hundred miles on both sides of the ocean. In mid-Atlantic, its only protection was a British battleship or armed merchant cruiser—a converted merchantman—to deal with surface raiders. But as the U-boats pressed westward, the convoys needed shore-to-shore protection from destroyers and corvettes, a requirement which spread the escorts very thin. A

convoy of 60 merchantmen required a shield of six or eight warships—and each warship spent up to one third of its life in refit. There was a high weather-damage rate because convoys sailed on schedule, regardless of storms.

In mid-1941 the Germans introduced wolf-pack tactics: submarines about 20 miles apart were organized into long patrol lines athwart the convoy routes. Each line had up to 20 U-boats and sometimes five or six lines were at sea at one time. All boats were controlled by radio from Adm. Karl Dönitz's headquarters in France. When a U-boat sighted a convoy, it radioed its position and shadowed the intended victims until the rest of the pack could be brought into striking range. Then the whole pack attacked, often at night, usually on the surface, from several directions. They sometimes got in among the merchant ships. Escorts were hard pressed to meet the attacks or to seek survivors of torpedoed ships.

In the first stage of the battle, Germany was fighting to cut Britain's lifeline. But after the United States entered the war, the U-boat crews knew they were fighting for larger stakes—to prevent the massing of an Allied invasion force in Britain. The number of U-boats available for operations in 1942 rose from 91 in January to 212 in December and the 1942 toll of shipping was 8,000,000 tons.

And the wolf packs grew ever stronger. In March 1943, they sank 627,000 tons—75 percent in convoy. Then, almost unexpectedly, the tide of battle was reversed. Convoys had more and more air protection, new support groups roamed the Atlantic, better radar and other anti-submarine weapons went into service. In one six-week period the U-boats suffered such heavy losses that Dönitz was forced to withdraw his battered fleet. It returned later but never again as a really serious threat.

This sudden and decisive Allied victory was won by brave men armed with a superb combination of vital tools of war—ships and weapons whose invention, development and production came to fruition in the Allies' hour of greatest need. It was in part a victory of Allied scientists over enemy scientists.

Mine Warfare

Among the serious early threats to Allied shipping were sea mines sown around Britain's harbors and in shallow coastal

waters by German submarines and surface vessels, or dropped by parachute. The tedious, dangerous job of clearing these mines was done by naval minesweepers. But scientists also sought ways to defend individual merchant ships.

The first sea mine was the contact mine, moored close to the surface by a cable attached to an anchor and exploded when hit by a passing ship. The Allies countered with a device called a paravane, which was towed on each side of the ship. When the towing wire struck a mooring cable, it guided the mine into a saw-toothed knife on the paravane which cut the mine from its cable. The mine floated to the surface and was destroyed by rifle or machine-gun fire.

In November 1939 the Germans introduced the magnetic mine. Dropped in shallow water by parachute, it settled on the seabed. As a ship passed over it, the magnetic field set up by the steel hull attracted the mine's magnetic needle, closing an electric circuit. This set off a detonator and exploded the mine's 650-pound charge under the ship. The Allies countered with a process known as degaussing: a cable was wrapped lengthwise around a ship and charged with electricity to reduce the magnetic field and enable the ship to pass over a mine without triggering the explosive mechanism. Later, degaussing was done by "wiping" an electric cable along a ship's sides.

The Germans then developed the acoustic mine, triggered by a microphone sensitive to a ship's water noises. The Allies countered noise with noise: an electrically driven hammer fitted to the bow beat against the ship's hull, producing a noise loud enough to explode the mine well ahead of the ship.

Both sides used mines. Allied ships and aircraft laid them in enemy-controlled coastal waters and harbors from the Bay of Biscay to Norway, and in the Baltic. Of 2340 enemy surface ships sunk by the Allies in the Atlantic and northwest European waters, about one third (759) were destroyed by air-laid mines. Some 48,000 mines were sown by the RAF and RCAF, almost 95 percent of them by Bomber Command.

The RCAF's No. 6 Bomber Group became particularly adept at laying mines—gardening, the aircrews called it—and was given responsibility for devising new techniques. Canadian Wellington squadrons equipped with radar navigation aids were

. . . when the weather was a mutual enemy, to us and the U-boats, the whole battle took on the recurring unreality of a nightmare.

Rear Adm. K. L. Dyer
in a foreword
to *50 North*
by Alan Easton

used as minelaying pathfinders. In the early years mines were usually dropped from heights under 6000 feet—a highly dangerous mission near a heavily defended port. In 1944 Allied scientists produced a new parachute mine that could be dropped accurately from 15,000 feet. The Canadians were the first to use it, over the inner harbor of Brest, France.

Compared to spectacular bombing raids, minelaying operations got little publicity. But the destruction of enemy shipping and the employment of hundreds of Germans on minesweeping and anti-aircraft defense made gardening one of the war's most valuable operations.

The U-boats

An Atlantic convoy's most prolific enemy was the Type VII U-boat. Some 700 were built in several variants, ranging from 600 to 1000 tons. The main one, the VII-C, had a radius of 6500 miles at 12 knots and a top surface speed of 17 knots. Its main drawback was its limited range.

As long as it operated close to Britain this was no problem, but when forced to operate in mid-Atlantic and along the North American coast, its patrol time was cut severely. The German answer was the Milch cow, a 1600-ton supply submarine with a range of 12,300 miles. It carried 720 tons of diesel oil in addition to its own supply. The Milch cow would rendezvous with a U-boat pack and deliver fuel, torpedoes, ammunition, fresh food and medical supplies. It would also take off sick and wounded crewmen and provide replacements.

The U-boat's slow underwater speed made it unsuitable as a full-scale submersible and the Germans used it as a diving torpedo boat. It traveled mostly on the surface, diving only to carry out daylight torpedo attacks or to evade enemy ships or aircraft. The U-boat's main power source was the diesel engines it used on the surface. Because they needed oxygen to operate, the diesels had to be shut off as soon as the boat dived. It then switched to electric motors driven by batteries good for

April 14, 1944: aboard the frigate *Swansea,* Canadian seamen search a German survivor from a U-boat sunk by an Atlantic support group. "This kill," Joseph Schull wrote in *The Far Distant Ships,* "had been a textbook action, its set movements so coldly and deliberately calculated that *Swansea's* commanding officer had had time to check his position by a leisurely sun sight while the hunt was in progress."

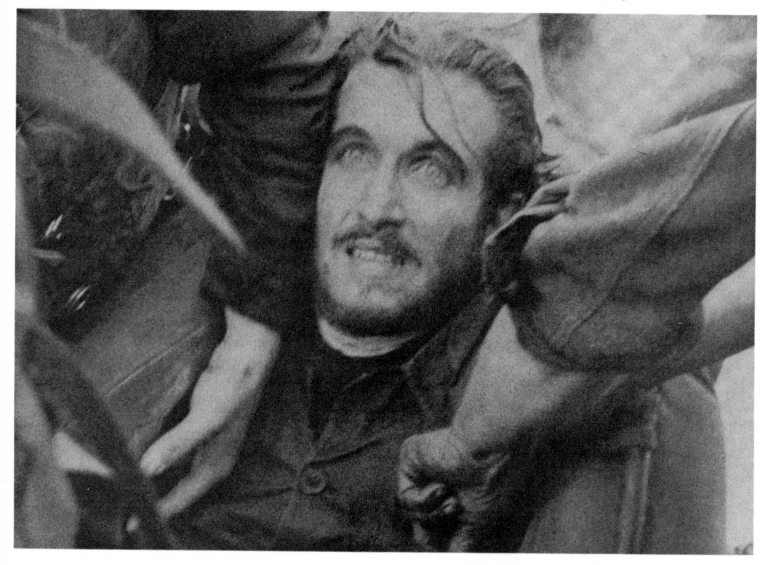

20 hours at four knots. After that the boat had to surface and use the diesels to recharge its batteries.

The U-boat's main armament consisted of 21-inch torpedoes, fired from tubes in the bow and stern. At first these were driven by compressed air, which left a telltale wake of white bubbles, often giving the intended victim time to evade. Later types were powered by electricity and the wake was almost invisible. In 1942 the U-boats were supplied with "circling" torpedoes. They ran zigzag, looping in and out of the convoy lines and greatly increasing the chances of a hit. But the greatest technical advance was the acoustic torpedo, which homed on the sound of a ship's propellers. Among its first victims, in September 1943, was the Canadian destroyer *St. Croix*. The Allies quickly countered with crude but effective noise-making devices towed 200 yards astern. They attracted the torpedo and detonated it harmlessly by generating noises louder than those of the ship's propellers.

The Escort Ships

Before the war the British Admiralty underestimated the U-boat threat. It believed the key weapon at sea would be the big-gunned warship and that German surface ships would be more dangerous than submarines. As a result, Britain did not build enough effective anti-submarine vessels. When war came she not only had too few warships to defend convoys, but those she could spare didn't have the endurance to cross the Atlantic as escorts.

To rectify this error, the navy called for a highly seaworthy, long-range escort ship, designed and equipped for anti-submarine warfare. What eventually emerged as the frigate was the real answer, but a stopgap substitute had to be found.

This was the corvette. Based on the design of a small whaler, corvettes could be built quickly and cheaply in small shipyards. They were constructed in Canada as well as Britain and many were manned by Canadian crews.

Although originally designed for patrolling coastal waters, corvettes operated as ocean escorts, and they proved far more seaworthy than the larger, more glamorous destroyers. Broad in beam and with a rounded stern which one Canadian skipper said was "inclined to turn up like a duck's tail," they could ride the heaviest seas, but had a vicious roll. And like the U-boats, they lacked adequate living space.

Not all corvettes were alike but a typical one was 190 feet long, had a speed of 16 knots and was armed with one 4-inch gun, two machine guns and 70 to 80 depth charges. In many ways the corvette was not very efficient for attacking U-boats. Its great advantage was a turning circle with a diameter of 200 yards—half the turning circle of a U-boat. A corvette therefore could maneuver to get depth charges in the right place ahead of a U-boat more accurately than a destroyer could. Corvette maneuverability also paid off in ramming attacks. Says Canadian naval historian Joseph Schull: "The Germans conceived a curiously exaggerated respect for these little warships. U-boats, although faster and with almost equal gunpower, never willingly attempted to fight it out with them on the surface."

Frigates eventually came into service in 1942. The River Class frigate—60 were built in Canada—was essentially a bigger and more formidable corvette: a 300-foot, 1400-ton twin-screw ship with a top speed of 19 knots. The frigate's endurance, 7200 miles at 12 knots, was twice that of the early Flower Class corvette. Armament included two 4-inch guns, automatic anti-aircraft weapons, 150 depth charges, the latest radar and eventually the hedgehog.

The Weapons

The early escorts had one basic weapons system: a listening device called asdic to detect a submerged submarine, and depth charges to destroy it. Asdic transmitted sound waves through the water; if they hit a submerged submarine, the echoes bounced back to the asdic receiver, producing a distinctive "pinging" noise. By calculating the time the sound waves took to go out and return, asdic could tell the U-boat's range and course. Having located the U-boat, the escort attacked with depth charges, steel cylinders containing some 300 pounds of explosives which could be preset to detonate at depths to 600 feet. The charges were dropped from rails at the escort's stern and projected by throwers to both sides of the ship so that they fell in a diamond pattern around the target.

The system had drawbacks. Asdic echoes were difficult to pick up in rough water and were deflected by water layers of different temperature. U-boats were sometimes able to escape by diving below this thermal layer. But asdic's most serious limitation was that, although it could pick up U-boat echoes from a mile away, it lost contact

when the escort came within 200 yards of the submerged boat. Thus, at the final stage of the attack, the escort had to aim its depth charges blind. During this period and in the time taken for the slow-sinking charges to explode, the U-boat could escape with a sharp alteration of course. Another problem was that the U-boat's pressure hull was so strong that a depth charge had to explode within 50 feet to damage the submarine. To place a charge that close was difficult—early asdic sets gave no indication of the U-boat's depth. Usually a submarine was destroyed not by a single direct hit but by the effect of many charges set to explode at different depths.

A breakthrough for the escorts came with the invention of the hedgehog. A multi-spigot mortar, it hurled 24 bombs in a wide oval pattern some 250 yards *ahead* of the ship so that asdic contact was maintained throughout the attack. The 65-pound hedgehog bombs, filled with a powerful new Torpex explosive, were fused to explode on contact and a direct hit was usually fatal. If the bombs missed, no near explosion took place to disturb asdic contact and the hedgehog would be reloaded for another attack.

By 1944 an even more deadly weapon called squid was in service. It fired three powerful time-fused projectiles ahead of the ship; they were aimed to explode around a U-boat and crack its hull by concussion. A near miss was often enough to destroy a submarine or force it to the surface. And a new asdic that detected submarine depth had been developed, making near misses and even direct hits more likely.

To locate surfaced submarines, the Allies relied on a high-frequency radio direction finder called Huff-Duff and on radar. U-boats used high-frequency radio to communicate with their home bases and with other boats in the wolf pack. To track the source of transmissions, the Allies set up Huff-Duff stations ashore. They took bearings on U-boat signals and passed the information on to the Admiralty in London. From the various bearings reported, a U-boat's position could be plotted and radioed to the convoy. Although the position was usually accurate only to within 50 miles, it enabled the convoy to take evasive action.

In 1942, scientists developed direction-finding sets small enough to be fitted in escort vessels. These sets picked up U-boat radio signals within 15 to 20 miles and, by taking bearings, escorts with Huff-Duff could fix a U-boat's position accurately.

Tactically, Huff-Duff robbed a patroling wolf pack of surprise for, in order to warn the pack of an approaching convoy, the U-boat which first sighted it had to break radio silence. By doing so it not only gave away its own position, but warned the convoy of a possible attack.

A major advance in detection came with shipborne search radar, an electronic "eye" that could locate submarines even through darkness and thick weather. Radar transmitted pulses of radio waves in a beam. A surfaced U-boat coming into the path of the beam reflected an echo back to the radar set where a device recorded the time the signal took to go out and return. Since radio waves travel at a constant 186,000 miles a second, the radar could establish the U-boat's position. The interception was recorded as a blip of light on the calibrated screen of a cathode ray tube. By following the blips, the radar operator could trace the U-boat's movements. The first shipboard set appeared in 1941. A crude affair with a masthead antenna turned by hand, it proved less than reliable.

The Germans countered radar with an equally cumbersome device called Metox, a radio receiver which picked up Allied signals with a manually rotated antenna set up in the conning tower after surfacing. The antenna had to be dismantled and moved below before the submarine could dive to escape an approaching escort ship.

In 1942, the Allies introduced a revolutionary radar employing the cavity magnetron, a small but extremely powerful transmitting tube. Operated on very short waves inaudible to Metox, it could detect a surfaced submarine from three to four miles and even locate one at periscope depth from a mile. Another valuable aid, the Plan Position Indicator, was linked to the ship's rotating radar antenna. The PPI showed all ships in the convoy area as dots of light. This not only revealed any submarine entering the area at night, but also enabled the escorts to keep station on the convoy and watch for stragglers. Radar was also installed in patroling Allied aircraft.

The Air-Sea War

Both sides used aircraft in the Battle of the Atlantic. The most formidable German plane, the Focke-Wulf Condor, was a long-range reconnaissance bomber, a military version of a prewar four-engine airliner. For its military role, Focke-Wulf engineers reinforced the fuselage, built in auxiliary fuel tanks and fitted bomb racks under the wings. But the FW 200 was not a true bomber. It was too slow, too vulnerable, and the bomb load of the first models was only 2000-3000 pounds. Nevertheless it did severe damage to Allied shipping in the early years. One of its first victims was the 42,000-ton liner *Empress of Britain*.

The Condor's prime role was reconnaissance. It had a radius of action of 1100 miles but if its bombs were replaced with extra fuel, it could fly 1475 miles into the Atlantic and return. It could shadow a convoy for several hours—endurance was 14 hours at 158 m.p.h.—and radio U-boats to intercept. Condors operating from Norway flew against Arctic convoys. They were supported by Heinkel 111 and Junkers 88 bombers which had a radius of some 560 miles. Fortunately for the convoys, the overcommitted Luftwaffe was never able to build its maritime arm to any great strength.

The Allied air-sea arm suffered at first from the same lack of endurance as the surface escorts. Establishment of air bases in Newfoundland and Iceland helped, but for a long time there was a mid-Atlantic gap in air protection. Improvement came after 1941 when Catalina flying boats, able to stay airborne for 17 hours, became available. They were followed by Very Long Range Liberator bombers (B24s).

Half of the 20 Liberators sent to RAF Coastal Command were soon lost through wastage and transfer to Ferry Command. Attempts to obtain more and to acquire long-range Lancaster bombers for Atlantic escorts failed. Instead the Allied High Command decided to bomb U-boat bases. It was a costly blunder.

The RAF-RCAF bomber force was diverted from attacks on Germany to strike at the massive concrete U-boat pens and building yards. From January to May 1943, at the height of the Atlantic battle, some 19,000 tons of bombs were dropped, more than 250 British, Canadian and American aircraft were lost and not a single U-boat was destroyed.

The convoys, meantime, sought to provide their own air protection. Each CAM ship (catapult-fitted merchant ship) carried a Hurricane fighter which was catapulted into the air as soon as an FW 200 was sighted. When the action was over, the Hurricane ditched beside the nearest merchant ship and the pilot hopefully was picked up.

Next came the auxiliary carriers. The dual-purpose MAC ships (merchant aircraft carriers) were oil tankers and grain ships fitted with a flight deck to carry three or four Swordfish aircraft. Much more formidable were the CVEs—small mass-produced escort carriers built on a merchant ship hull and topped by a long wooden flight deck. When the first of these 15,000-ton carriers sailed with a convoy in March 1943, the mid-Atlantic's air gap was finally closed.

Eventually more than a hundred CVEs were built; two, *Nabob* and *Puncher,* were manned by Canadians. The number of aircraft carried by CVEs varied, but *Nabob* had 12 Avenger torpedo-bombers for anti-submarine operations and four Wildcat V fighter planes.

Aircraft proved to be highly effective anti-submarine weapons. Their speed and range of vision were superior to those of surface escorts, and an aircraft had only to circle a convoy to force any U-boat within striking distance to submerge, thus crippling its ability to attack. The capacity of aircraft to search out and kill was further increased with the introduction in 1943 of airborne radar based on the cavity magnetron. Now an aircraft could track down U-boats by night as well as day. At night it used its radar to home on a surfaced U-boat and, on reaching the target, switched on a powerful searchlight called the Leigh Light. By day, the radar-guided aircraft surprised surfaced U-boats by diving out of the sun or from heavy cloud. And even if the attack failed, the aircraft could home surface escorts onto the targets. Eventually the Germans came up with a receiver called Naxos to detect Allied radar signals and enable U-boats to take evasive action. But the supremacy of aircraft over the U-boat is demonstrated by the records; of 705 U-boats sunk in the Atlantic, the Arctic and British waters, 302 were destroyed by planes.

The Hunter-Killers

Until 1943 an escort group commander faced a dilemma whenever he learned U-boats were tailing his convoy: could he use warships to hunt the U-boats and still have enough left to ensure the safety of the convoy? The answer was usually no.

In the spring of 1943 the situation changed. Frigates and other escorts which had supported the invasion of North Africa were now available for duty in the North Atlantic. The RN and RCN at last had enough strength to form support groups. Known also as hunter-killer groups, they usually consisted of six vessels not tied to a specific convoy but free to race to the rescue of any threatened by wolf-pack attack. While the convoy's escort ships sailed on, the support group sought out the U-boats and attacked until they were either destroyed or forced to surface because their batteries and air supply were exhausted.

In April and May the Allies unleashed six support groups in the North Atlantic and, with their arrival, the tide of battle swiftly turned. By May the wolf packs were forced to withdraw to their bases. From then on Allied sea and air escorts grew so strong that, although the U-boats returned in September, they were never able to regain the initiative.

The Last Fling

Technically the Germans were still far from defeated. Because he could no longer deploy his boats successfully on the surface, Admiral Dönitz realized he must create a fast and agile underwater U-boat fleet. By mid-1943 plans to build such a fleet were

six knots, making it difficult to get into position for attack. Operating at periscope depth also restricted vision.

Meanwhile German technicians were working on a revolutionary submarine called the Walther-boat. It was driven by gas turbines which used a new fuel consisting mainly of hydrogen peroxide. It had a streamlined hull and promised to operate totally submerged at 20 to 25 knots. But it was still only experimental.

More to the moment was the new Type XXI—a 1600-ton, schnorkel-equipped U-boat rushed into production straight from the drawing board, without undergoing prototype tests. Although driven by conventional diesel-electric motors, the Type XXI carried massive electric batteries which gave a top *submerged* speed of 16 knots. Its surface range was 11,150 miles at 12 knots. The Type XXI had many new features: its schnorkel was covered with a synthetic coating that made it immune to radar detection; a warning receiver could detect all Allied radar signals; in addition to

jet aircraft, Germany's new submarine had come too late.

Canada played a vital role in the Battle of the Atlantic. At the battle's peak the RCN directed the anti-submarine war in the whole northwest Atlantic—and the RCAF's Eastern Air Command was responsible for air protection there. Later the navy directed operations for the entire North Atlantic. The real measure of the RCN achievement was not the 27 U-boats it sank or helped sink but the fact that by far the largest proportion of the shipments it guarded got through. In addition, Eastern Air Command crews sank six submarines and damaged three; Canadian squadrons in RAF Coastal Command destroyed 16.

Canada's warships fought in many phases of the global sea war—off the coasts of Europe, on the harsh runs to Murmansk in Russia, in landings in western Europe and the Mediterranean. While mainly a small-ship navy, the RCN manned, commissioned and operated vessels of many types, from

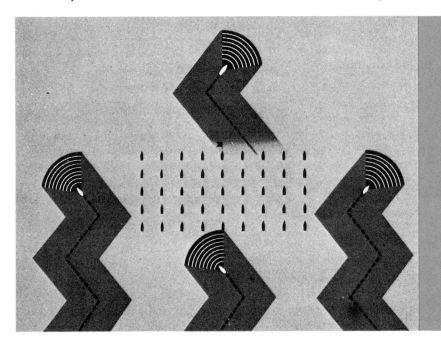

ATLANTIC CONVOY

A destroyer and three corvettes guard 45 merchant ships (nine columns of five ships each) in this convoy illustration. These 45 ships, if sailed independently, would make 45 targets—and require at least 45 escorting warships. Sailed in convoy, they become a single target, each running much less risk of being detected and sunk by a U-boat, and they can be adequately protected by far fewer escorts. The corvettes, on the flanks and astern, come under the orders of the senior officer of the escort, in the destroyer in front. All four maintain an asdic watch and steer a zigzag course to make maximum use of their anti-submarine capabilities. The convoy commodore, probably a former naval officer called back from retirement, flies his flag in the leading ship of the center column. The biggest convoy of the war had 167 ships and covered about 30 square miles.

ready. In the meantime Dönitz had a stop-gap weapon—the schnorkel.

Essentially the schnorkel was a breathing apparatus. An air tube incorporating a float valve projected just above the water and enabled the U-boat to draw in air to run its diesel engines. A second pipe discharged the exhaust fumes. Using schnorkel, a submarine could cruise unseen at periscope depth and charge its batteries without surfacing. But although schnorkel enabled a U-boat to stay under water for many days (the record was 66), it could move at only

acoustic torpedoes, it carried a new torpedo which set its own course to the target, making toward it in a series of sweeping turns. Six could be fired in one salvo from tubes in the bow. There were also six tubes both port and starboard.

The Type XXI was a powerful weapon but Allied bombing raids in 1944 delayed its construction. The first of these submarines did not go on patrol until the end of April 1945. A week later Germany capitulated and the order went out to all U-boats to surrender. Like her rocket missiles and

local patrol craft through sleek motor torpedo boats, minesweepers, corvettes, frigates, destroyers and eventually two cruisers. There were several flotillas of Canadian landing craft and two infantry landing ships. Canadians also manned two Royal Navy escort carriers and more than 4000 Canadians served on loan with the Royal Navy. But it was in the bitter Battle of the Atlantic that Canadian seamen made their crucial contribution to Allied victory.

CRUISER

Armament included nine 6-inch guns, eight 4-inch guns, three 2-pounder pom-pom guns, eight twin Oerlikon and six single Oerlikon guns, torpedoes fired from six 21-inch tubes. Displacement, 8000 tons; length, 555 feet; top speed, 31 knots; crew, 700 to 905.

The largest RCN ship of the war was the cruiser *Uganda*. Commissioned in 1944, she sailed for the Far East in December, the first of 60 ships Canada intended to send to the Pacific to support the war against Japan. In fact, *Uganda* was the only Canadian ship to see Pacific action, sailing with the United States Fifth Fleet in operations against Okinawa, and with the British Fleet. A second Canadian cruiser, *Ontario,* served in the Pacific.

ESCORT CARRIER

Ship details, planes and armament varied. The following refers to *Nabob:* Two 5-inch guns, 16 40-mm. guns, 20 20-mm. guns, 12 Avenger torpedo-bombers and four Wildcat fighter planes. Displacement, 15,000 tons; length, 495 feet; top speed, 18 knots; crew, more than 800.

The mid-Atlantic, beyond the range of land-based aircraft, was the U-boats' favorite killing ground until the Allies found a way to give convoys air protection from shore to shore. They did so with the escort carrier, a merchant hull with a long wooden flight deck. Mass produced in U.S. shipyards—more than 100 were built—they also gave air support on landing operations. Canada manned two—*Nabob* and *Puncher*—with the Royal Navy providing pilots and service crews.

TRIBAL CLASS DESTROYER

Three twin 4.7-inch guns, twin 4-inch high-angle guns, six twin 20-mm. Oerlikon guns, 11 close-range automatic weapons, 21-inch torpedoes fired from four tubes, depth charges, hedgehog spigot mortar. Displacement, 1927 tons; length, 377 feet; top speed, 36 knots; crew, about 250.

Most Canadian destroyers were used chiefly to escort convoys. Not so the RCN's four Tribals. Virtually pocket cruisers, they were fast, powerfully armed vessels whose main role was to seek out and destroy enemy ships. *Athabaskan, Iroquois, Haida* and *Huron* formed part of the highly successful 10th Destroyer Flotilla operating off France in 1944. During one five-month period that year, the flotilla sank 36 ships and damaged 15 others. *Athabaskan* was lost by enemy action.

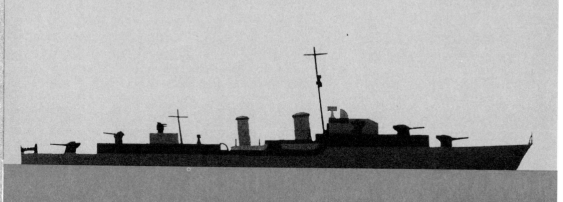

TOWN CLASS DESTROYER

Ship details and armament varied. A typical four-stacker was some 300 feet long, displaced 1060 tons, and had a top speed of 28 knots. Armament included 4-inch guns, automatic anti-aircraft guns, and torpedoes fired from 21-inch tubes. Some were fitted with the hedgehog mortar as well as depth charges.

In 1940, when German invasion seemed imminent, Britain received 50 destroyers from the United States in the famous ships-for-bases deal. Canada was given seven of them. Built in 1919-20, the narrow-beamed four-stackers were hard ships to handle even in light seas. To improve stability they were stripped of much of their original armament and after refit gave fine service. Six survived. *St. Croix* was torpedoed in 1943.

RIVER CLASS FRIGATE

Two 4-inch guns, one 12-pounder gun, four twin 20-mm. Oerlikon guns, 150 depth charges launched from rails and throwers, a hedgehog spigot mortar forward. Displacement, 1400 tons; length, 300 feet; top speed, 19 knots; crew, 140 to 160.

The frigate, specially designed as an anti-submarine vessel, was faster and better armed than the corvette. Canada built and manned 60 of these twin-screw, 19-knot ships and 10 British-built frigates served with the RCN. Frigates were used to escort convoys and in support groups whose task was to hunt down submarines. One Canadian frigate, *Swansea,* shared three U-boat kills.

FLOWER CLASS CORVETTE

Ship details varied. The following refers to a 1943 Revised Flower Class corvette built to give an increased endurance of 7400 miles at 10 knots: One 4-inch gun, one 2-pounder pom-pom gun, two 20-mm. Oerlikon guns, 70 depth charges launched from rails and throwers, a hedgehog spigot mortar forward. Displacement, 970 tons; length, 208 feet; top speed, 16 knots; crew, 80 to 90.

The rugged little corvette bore the brunt of Canada's war with the U-boats, and of the 122 that served with the RCN ten were lost in action. The original Flower Class ships had an open deck between the forecastle and the bridge superstructure. This was a man-killer in bad weather and in later ships the forecastle deck was extended to abreast of the funnel (as here). Canada built 106 Flower Class corvettes, many of them in shipyards along the Great Lakes.

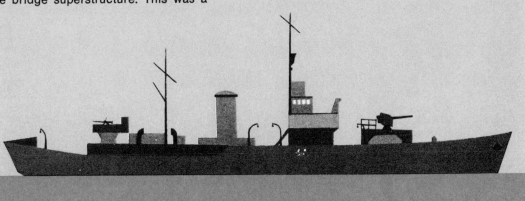

BANGOR MINESWEEPER

Typical armament: one 12-pounder gun, one twin and two single Oerlikons, 40 depth charges launched from rails and throwers. Displacement, 672 tons; length, 180 feet; top speed, 16 knots; crew, 80.

The basic task of the sweeper was to clear coastal waters and harbor approaches of enemy mines. But most of Canada's Bangors were ordered to leave sweeping gear ashore and were used instead to escort convoys, chiefly in the St. Lawrence and on the triangle run—St. John's, Halifax, Boston and New York. Sixteen Canadian Bangors took part in the Normandy D-Day landing, plodding ahead of the invasion armada to clear mines and mark the swept channels with buoys—all within range of enemy guns.

MOTOR TORPEDO BOAT

The RCN operated two types of MTB. The 29th Flotilla had the 71-foot G Type (shown here) which had a top speed of 41 knots; the 65th Flotilla used the 110-foot D Type with a maximum of 30 knots. Both were armed with a 6-pounder pom-pom gun and small automatics. Normally they carried torpedoes, but during the invasion some boats exchanged these for depth charges.

Canada had two flotillas of MTBs—small, swift, highly agile attack boats designed to operate in shallow waters. Formed in 1944, they served with British Coastal Forces in the English Channel, carrying out night attacks on enemy coastal shipping and sometimes fighting running battles with German torpedo boats and tangling with destroyers. On and after D-Day they served as escorts and helped guard the flanks of the invasion beaches and blockade enemy harbors.

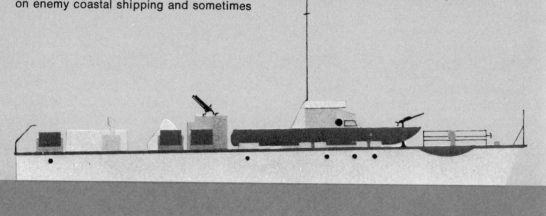

FAIRMILE MOTOR LAUNCH

Armament varied, but a typical Fairmile mounted one 3-pounder gun forward and machine guns aft. About 20 depth charges were carried, some craft being fitted with a double-barreled Y gun which fired two depth charges simultaneously, one to each side of the boat. Displacement, 79 tons; length, 112 feet; top speed, 20 knots; crew, 16.

One of the smallest of the RCN's fighting ships was the Fairmile, a wooden launch powered by two 630-h.p. gasoline engines. The Fairmiles' mad pitching and tossing earned them the name Holy Rollers. Operating usually in flotillas of six, they were used chiefly for anti-submarine patrols off the Canadian coast. Some of the 128 Fairmiles manned by Canadians served in the Mediterranean, running a ferry service which supplied arms to Greek partisans on German-held islands.

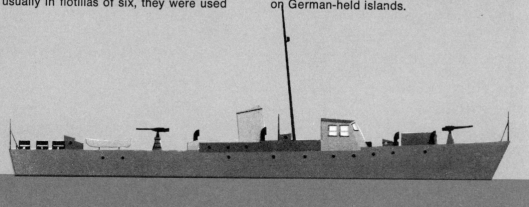

LANDING SHIP INFANTRY

Canada's *Prince David* and *Prince Henry* were pre-war liners converted to armed merchant cruisers and refitted in 1943 as LSIs (Landing Ships Infantry). They carried 550 troops, six LCAs and two LCMs (below)—the landing craft being launched a few miles from shore. Armament included two twin-mounted 4-inch guns, two Bofors and ten Oerlikon guns. Length, 385 feet; top speed, 22 knots; naval crew, 250.

During World War II an armada of strange new vessels was developed. Called landing craft, they were designed to disgorge men, tanks, guns and supplies directly onto enemy-held beaches, from staging areas hundreds of miles away. Small-scale commando raids gave the Allies their first chance to experiment with assault craft. Then, in August 1942, some 200 landing-craft carriers took part in the Canadian raid on Dieppe. It was a costly trial by fire but it taught the Allies vital lessons for the Mediterranean landings and for the great amphibious D-Day assault in Normandy.

LANDING CRAFT ASSAULT

LCAs were lightly armored 41-foot wooden vessels designed to land some 30 assault troops directly onto a beach.

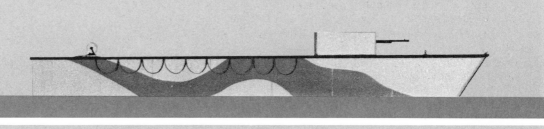

LANDING CRAFT MECHANIZED

Steel-hulled LCMs were 50 feet long and fitted with a ramp bow. They carried men, jeeps and light tracked vehicles. All landing craft had light machine guns.

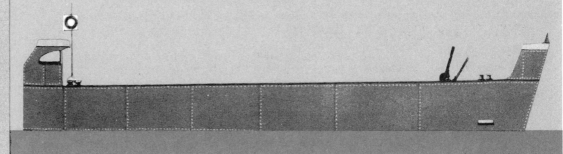

LANDING CRAFT INFANTRY

Designed and built in the United States, the Landing Craft Infantry (Large) had an endurance of some 6000 miles and could sail on a long passage before landing troops on an assault beach. In addition to her own crew she carried 150 soldiers below decks. She was armed with three to four 20-mm. cannon, was 158 feet long and had a top speed of 12 knots.

Canada provided 10,000 men and 110 ships—destroyers, corvettes, minesweepers and motor torpedo boats—for the Normandy landings of June 1944. On D-Day itself, assault craft of *Prince David* and *Prince Henry* landed some of the first Canadian and British troops. Close behind, under their own power, came 30 Landing Craft Infantry of three Canadian flotillas. Despite difficulties, the landings went well. The Canadian flotillas put 4600 men ashore on D-Day, and although many craft were damaged, not one Canadian sailor was killed.

NO DAY, NO NIGHT, NO SEASON . . .

U-boat commander Wolfgang Lüth, at a German naval officers' course in 1943:

A man being depth-charged in a U-boat is like an airman being attacked by three fighters at once. He can hear every "shot" and, whether or not the shot strikes home, the sound of it makes him shrink. But the U-boat man cannot fly away; he cannot move or return the fire. Often the lights go out and in the dark everyone feels more afraid.

Life in a U-boat is unnatural and unhealthy. There is no sharp distinction between night and day or even the seasons, and the normal rhythm of life is reduced to an even monotony. Even the fittest and healthiest suffer under the changes of climate: the boat passes from the trade winds to the tropics, from damp and cold into the atmosphere of summer.

The fog on board gets on your nerves. The perpetual din, the movement of the boat. The effects of drinking strong coffee and too much smoking are bad for the stomach and nerves. I have seen lads of 23, after two years of it, become unfit for seagoing service.

Because night and day tend to merge, the commander must try to restore the distinction artificially. During supper I have the lights dimmed throughout the boat and for an hour every evening we have a concert on gramophone records. The difference between Sunday and weekdays is also underlined. We start Sunday with a concert and the first record is always the same: "Till ten o'clock it's my Sunday treat to stay in bed and rest my feet." And the last record of the day is also the same but something better: *"Abendlied,"* sung by the choirboys of Regensburg Cathedral.

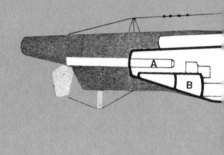

The men must know what they are fighting for and they must consciously and willingly stake their lives for it. On Sundays I sometimes dive deep and hold a general muster of the crew. I tell them of the Reich and the great figures of our history and the contributions they have made.

From *U-Boats at War,* by Harald Busch

STRICTLY CHORE SHIPS

"They rolled, they bucked, they bounced," William H. Pugsley wrote of corvettes, "until men were dazed, shaken and utterly worn out." But they did the job, these ships that were the symbol of Canada in the Battle of the Atlantic. From Pugsley's descriptions of corvette life, in his book *Saints, Devils and Ordinary Seamen:*

"All small ships' messdecks are much the same. There's the seamen's mess forward, with the stokers usually just underneath. Other ratings' messes may be tucked away in other parts of the ship but the seamen live in the forecastle, the least comfortable part, as they have for generations. Along the inside of the hull run lockers for clothes; above them are racks for boots, attaché cases and cap boxes. The lockers are low enough to make a settee, beside which is the mess table, firmly bolted to the deck. On the other side is a bench. Set in the low deckhead (ceiling) are hooks for hammocks. Nearby there's a rack for stowing them in daytime and a cabinet for the mess cutlery, chinaware, utensils and staples like tea, butter, sugar and tinned milk."

Pugsley paid this tribute to the men in corvette engine rooms: "If the ship is torpedoed, the boys at the boilers—and there are always some there—almost never get out. If they aren't killed by the actual explosion, they die when water rushes in and the boilers blow up. There they work, far below decks in a maze of hissing valves and clanking pumps, surrounded by pipes of live steam which in escaping can be more deadly than any bullet. They're hemmed in by thin walls, with the whole ocean pressing to enter. They know that if the ship comes off second best in a duel with a submarine, they'll never have time to make the long awkward climb to the upper deck. This thought is with them too when the ship in heavy seas keeps trying to roll herself right over. It takes guts to be a stoker."

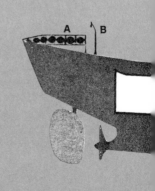

The RCN had bigger ships, wrote Pugsley, "ships that went out on more glamorous missions, but they carried no stouter hearts. The corvettes went everywhere, from the ice-filled Strait of Belle Isle to the bullet-swept beaches of North Africa, from the sunless fjords of Iceland to the tropic roadstead of Aruba. Strictly chore ships."

The Type VIIC U-boat (this one with a 37-mm. anti-aircraft gun replacing the original 3.5-inch main-deck weapon) was the Germans' principal weapon at midwar. Its main features: (A) stern torpedo tube, (B) electric motors and torpedo storage, (C) diesel motors, (D) galley, (E) escape hatch, (F) electric batteries, (G) crew space, (H) 37-mm. gun, (I) four 20-mm. guns, (J) control position for both search and attack periscopes, (K) hatch to conning tower, (L) officers' quarters, (M) crew space and torpedo storage, (N) four torpedo tubes.

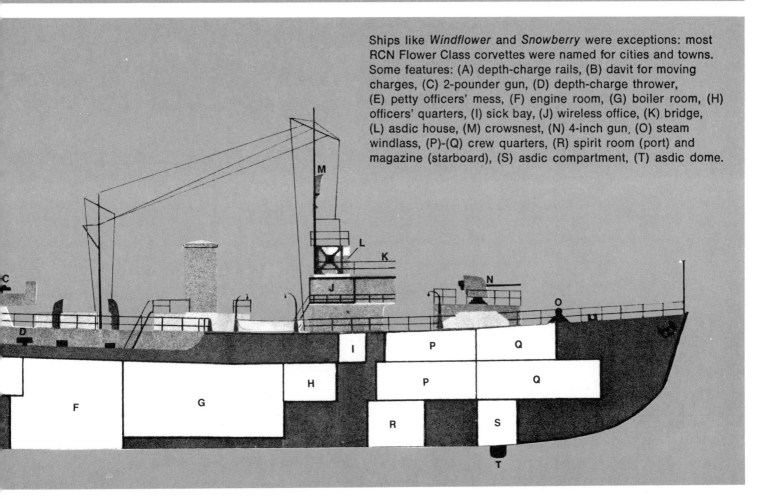

Ships like *Windflower* and *Snowberry* were exceptions: most RCN Flower Class corvettes were named for cities and towns. Some features: (A) depth-charge rails, (B) davit for moving charges, (C) 2-pounder gun, (D) depth-charge thrower, (E) petty officers' mess, (F) engine room, (G) boiler room, (H) officers' quarters, (I) sick bay, (J) wireless office, (K) bridge, (L) asdic house, (M) crowsnest, (N) 4-inch gun, (O) steam windlass, (P)-(Q) crew quarters, (R) spirit room (port) and magazine (starboard), (S) asdic compartment, (T) asdic dome.

TYPE IIB: THE TRAINING U-BOAT

When Germany began re-arming in the mid-'30s she aimed at building 300 U-boats by 1943. Hitler pushed her into war faster than the navy anticipated, and in 1939 she had only some 60 submarines, about the same as the British. Half were Type IIs, small coastal U-boats used mainly for training. Type IIB: displacement, 279 tons; length, 140 feet; speed, 13 knots (7 knots submerged); six 21-inch torpedoes fired from three tubes forward; one 20-mm. gun; crew, 25.

TYPE IX: THE LONG-RANGE RAIDER

The most formidable of ocean-going U-boats were the Type IX variants which ranged from 1000 to 1600 tons. Because of their excellent speed and range they were used not only as attack boats but as long-distance minelayers and submarine supply tankers. The largest was the Type IXD/2: displacement, 1616 tons; length, 287 feet; speed, 19 knots (7 submerged); range, 23,700 miles at 12 knots; six 21-inch tubes (24 torpedoes); one 4.1-inch, one 37-mm., one 20-mm. gun; crew, 57.

TYPE VIIC: THE MAINSTAY OF THE FLEET

The most common enemy of RCN ships guarding the convoys was the Type VII U-boat. Most had a range of only 6500 miles but could extend their patrol by refueling at sea from Milch cow supply submarines. The leading raider at the peak of the battle in 1942-43 was the VIIC: displacement, 769 tons; length, 220 feet; speed, 17 knots (7 knots submerged); 14 21-inch torpedoes fired from four tubes forward, one aft; one 3.5-inch (later one 37-mm.), two 20-mm. guns; crew, 44.

TYPE XXI: THE UNTESTED KILLER

After its heavy losses in 1943, the U-boat fleet hoped to regain supremacy with the sleek, powerfully-armed Type XXI. Designed to operate fully submerged, it had a top speed of 16 knots—underwater as well as on the surface. But production was delayed by air raids on building yards and the war ended before any saw action. Displacement, 1600 tons; length, 251 feet; range, 11,150 miles at 12 knots; 18 21-inch torpedo tubes; four 30-mm. guns; crew, 57.

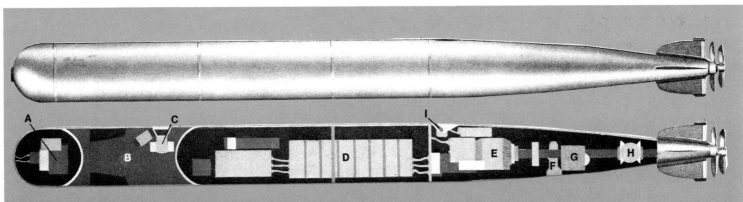

THE 21-INCH TORPEDO

The U-boat's main weapon was the torpedo. About 18 feet long and 21 inches in diameter, it was launched from a torpedo tube by a blast of compressed air, then propelled through the water by its own motor. Torpedoes had an average range of five miles at 40 knots but were most effective at two to three miles. One hit was often enough to send a ship of 10,000 tons to the bottom.

The early torpedo was launched on a preset course and guided by a gyrocompass. Driven by compressed air, it left a telltale trail of bubbles, but this problem was later overcome by equipping the torpedo with an electric motor.

In September 1943 the Germans introduced the acoustic torpedo (above). Designed to home on noises from a ship's propellers, it was guided to its target by two hydrophones and an automatic steering device in the nose (A). Behind the nose compartment was a 600-pound explosive warhead (B)

and a firing pistol (C). The next section contained an electric battery (D) which drove the motor (E). Behind this was the depth control gear (F), gyroscopic stabilizer (G), differential gear (H) and tail unit and propellers. As the torpedo was fired, a starting lever (I) set the motor in motion. When the hydrophones picked up a ship's noises, it diverted from its course and headed straight for the ship, exploding on contact.

The countermeasure—called cat gear by the Canadian Navy—was simple but effective: two iron bars, separated by rubber spacers, which banged against each other when towed some 200 yards behind the ship. Making a noise far louder than the ship's screws—one U-boat man said the sound was "like a power saw in labor"—the cat gear attracted the torpedo, causing it to explode harmlessly well astern of the ship.

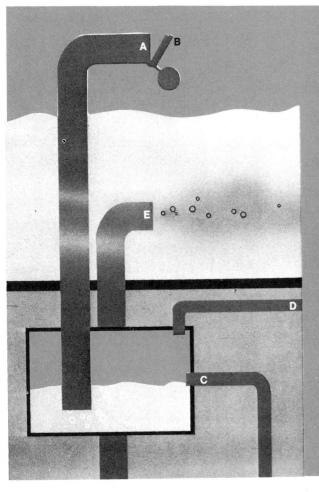

THE SCHNORKEL

From summer 1943 on, ever-increasing patrols by Allied radar-equipped planes and escort ships forced the U-boat fleet to operate under water. Since a U-boat needed oxygen to run its diesel engines, it had to travel on its battery-driven electric motors when submerged. These were good for about 20 hours at four knots, after which the U-boat had to surface to recharge the batteries with its diesels. Robbed of speed and mobility, the U-boat lost its sting.

The long-term answer lay in building submarines that could operate entirely under water. In the meantime the Germans came up with a stopgap, the schnorkel breathing tube. This device enabled a U-boat to run submerged at periscope depth on its diesels and to recharge its batteries without surfacing. As this diagram shows, the schnorkel consisted of an air induction tube (A) protruding a few feet above the sea, with a float valve (B) to prevent water entering. If water got in before the valve fully closed, it was held in a water chamber and drawn off through a drain pipe (C). When the diesels were started, air was drawn down the induction tube into the water chamber and through another tube (D) to the engines. Some of the fresh air was also used to replenish the submarine's oxygen supply. Diesel exhaust fumes were discharged into the sea through an exhaust pipe (E).

The schnorkel enabled a U-boat to travel submerged for days on end and gave it some security from Allied radar. But the submarine's attack capability was still greatly limited. Operating at periscope depth restricted its vision and, even with its diesels, it could run under water at only six knots—slower than the ships it was sent to destroy.

DEPTH CHARGE

When Allied escort ships attacked a U-boat they used an underwater listening device called asdic (see opposite page) to locate the submarine and depth charges to destroy it. The depth charge (A) was a steel cylinder containing some 300 pounds of explosive and could be preset to detonate at depths to 600 feet. When the charge reached the preset depth, water pressure activated a firing pistol (B) which set off an explosive primer (C) and detonated the charge.

Depth charges were dropped from rails at the stern of the ship, and were projected to port and starboard by throwers (right) on each side. The depth charge rested on a carrier (D) which fitted into the barrel of the thrower. When the order to fire was given, the operator pulled a firing handle (E) which fired the propellant cartridge inside the barrel. This hurled the charge some 75 yards abeam, with the carrier (F) falling separately into the sea.

The charges were dropped and thrown around the target in a diamond pattern (right) and sank at about ten feet a second. Usually a U-boat was destroyed not by a direct hit but by the cumulative effect of several near explosions which eventually cracked the hull.

Finding and killing a U-boat was far from easy. They too had listening gear and some German captains became very adept at evasive action. They sometimes used a decoy called *Pillenwerfer* (pill thrower). This device ejected chemical pellets which produced clouds of bubbles to simulate a U-boat's wake and lead a hunter astray. But the most serious problems for an Allied anti-submarine ship were the big limitations imposed by its own weapons. Because asdic was ineffective at short ranges, an attacker lost contact with the U-boat when she got close enough to drop depth charges. After an attack, the exploding charges and the attacker's wake so churned the water that asdic contact could not be quickly regained. An answer came in 1942 with the invention of a weapon called hedgehog.

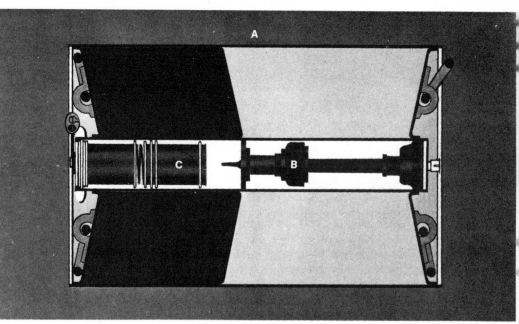

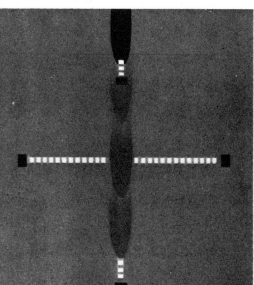

HEDGEHOG

Hedgehog was an electrically-fired spigot mortar mounted on the forecastle of an escort ship. It consisted of a steel platform with rows of spigots projecting like the spines on a hedgehog's back. The 65-pound hedgehog projectile (A) was loaded onto a spigot and fired by an electrical contact. This set off a primer inside an explosive cartridge (B), hurling the projectile forward. When it hit the target, a percussion fuse (C) set off exploder pellets (D) and detonated the bomb. The rows of spigots were angled so that the bombs fell around the U-boat in an oval pattern.

The hedgehog's advantage was that it hurled its 24 contact-fused bombs some 250 yards *ahead* of the ship, enabling the escort to keep in asdic contact with the U-boat throughout the attack and give more accurate fire. But if the bombs missed, no explosions occurred to disturb the asdic echoes, and the hedgehog could be reloaded for another try.

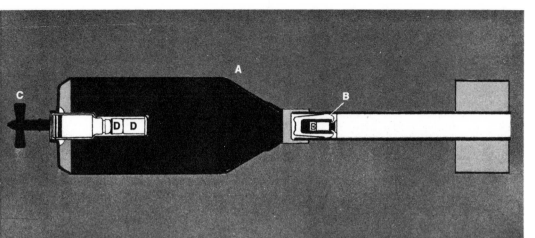

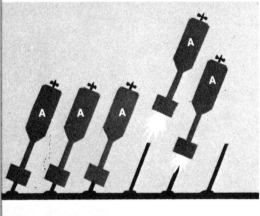

ASDIC

The asdic underwater listening device got its name from the Allied Submarine Detection Investigation Committee which developed the first model during World War I. Asdic consisted of a transmitter-receiver which sent sound impulses through the water. If the sound waves hit a submerged U-boat the echoes bounced back to the asdic receiver. The time taken for the signals to go out and the echoes to return was calculated to give the U-boat's range—the shorter the time, the closer the target. By plotting the changing ranges, the escort could track the U-boat's course.

Asdic signals were transmitted from a dome under the ship. Three impulse waves were sent out: the wide beam swept in slow stages around the ship to seek out the U-boat; the other beams fixed the U-boat's position accurately once it was located. Asdic could normally detect a U-boat at 1500 yards and track it accurately to within about 200 yards.

BOFORS GUN

The Bofors 40-mm. automatic anti-aircraft gun was a Swedish design adopted and manufactured under license by many nations and was widely used on land and at sea. The gun was fed by chargers, each holding four rounds, which were placed into hopper loading guides above the breech. With a 360-degree traverse and 90-degree elevation, it could track a target without interruption. The effective altitude range was 12,000 feet. Bofors mounted singly had a crew of six. Twin- and quadruple-mounted Bofors had extra men for loading and were controlled by a gun director.

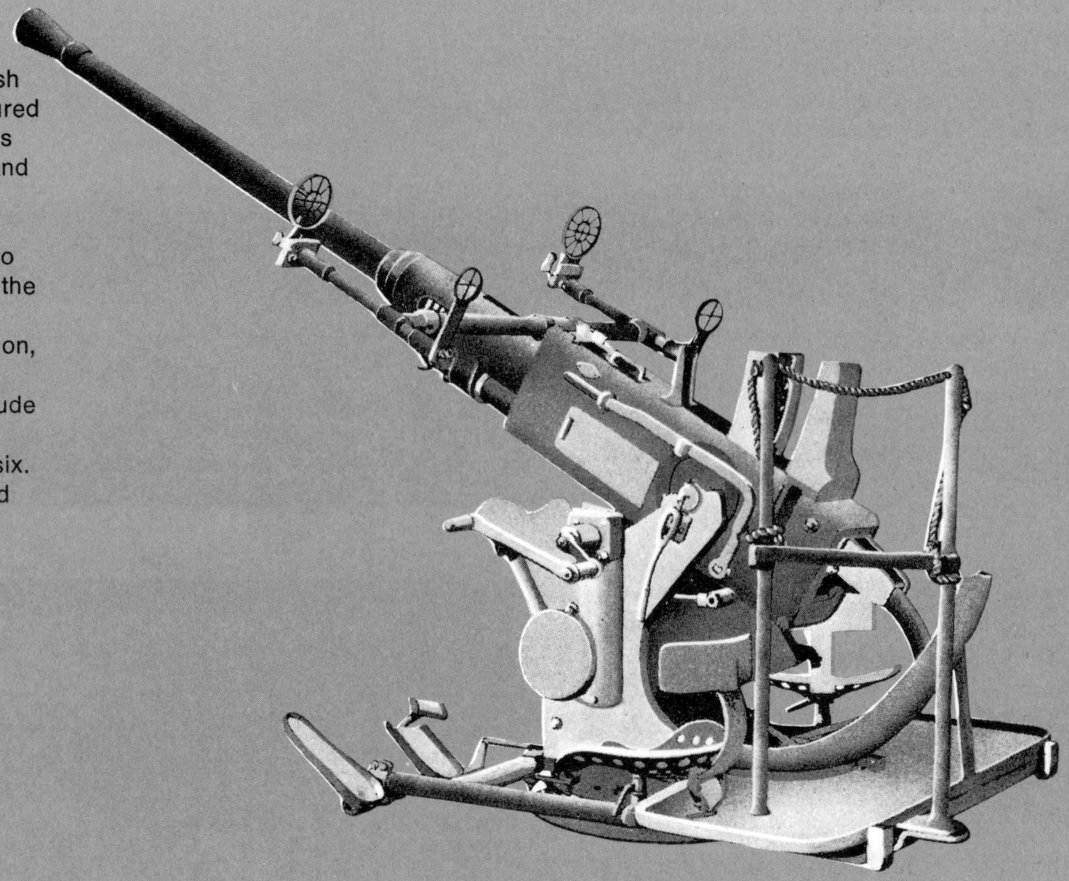

4-INCH NAVAL GUN

The 4-inch gun was the standard weapon for surface action in RCN minesweepers, corvettes, frigates and destroyers. The breech-loading gun shown here needed a separate charge and projectile; the quick-firing type used fixed ammunition (combined charge and projectile). In small craft the guns were in local control, but in larger ships they were controlled by directors on the bridge or superstructure. The 4-inch fired high explosive, semi-armor piercing and starshell and had a range of eight miles. It could be used against aircraft.

HOTCHKISS MACHINE GUN

Mounted in ships, the British Hotchkiss light machine gun was used for anti-aircraft defense. An air-cooled, gas-operated gun, it fired .303 cartridges and was fed by tempered metal strips holding 30 rounds. The Mark I* also accepted a metal link belt holding 50 rounds.

LEWIS MACHINE GUN

The .303 Lewis, used in World War I, was Canada's standard light machine gun until replaced by the Bren in 1939. The navy used it as an anti-aircraft gun. Gas-operated, it could be fired only in full automatic. The rotating pan magazine held 47 rounds.

BROWNING GUN

The anti-aircraft model of the Browning .50 machine gun was a water-cooled, belt-fed weapon with a rate of fire of 400 rounds a minute. Mounted in pairs on a pedestal, the Browning was widely fitted in merchant ships and coastal craft.

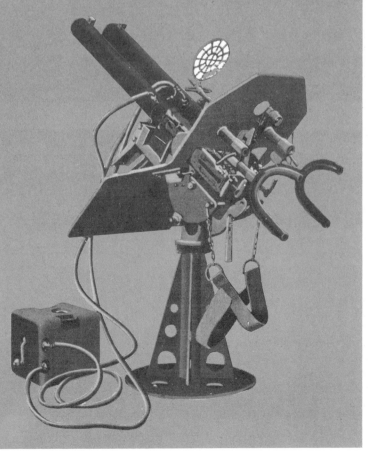

OERLIKON 20-mm. CANNON

The Oerlikon automatic, designed for high-angle, close-range anti-aircraft fire, was mounted in all types of vessels from coastal craft to battleships. Firing explosive bullets, it was fed by a 60-round drum magazine. The twin version had a power-operated turret.

MAGNETIC MINE

Both sides waged war with mines: offensively to destroy ships in enemy harbors and coastal waters, defensively to protect home waters from enemy raiders. Mines were sown by minelaying ships, submarines and aircraft and were of three types: contact mines which exploded when hit, and magnetic and acoustic mines.

The magnetic mine (right) was dropped in shallow water by aircraft, and as it fell the two-piece nose cone (A) parted to release a parachute. On hitting the water, the parachute detached and the mine fell to the seabed where it was secured by its anti-roll horns (B). When a ship passed, the vessel's magnetic field attracted a magnetic needle in the mine (C). This closed an electrical contact which set off a detonator and exploded the mine's 650-pound charge directly under the ship.

The Germans began sowing magnetic mines around Britain in the first week of the war and by the end of 1939 they had sunk 79 ships and a destroyer. The mine was touted as "Hitler's secret weapon" but it had been used by the British in 1918. The Allies countered it by equipping ships with a degaussing girdle —an electrically charged cable fitted around a ship which reduced its magnetic field so that it could pass over a mine without triggering the firing mechanism.

ACOUSTIC MINE

Acoustic mines were introduced by the Germans in late 1940. They were usually sown by minelaying submarines which stole into harbor approaches, dropped the mines through tubes and left without being seen. The mine was set off by battery-operated microphones (A) which picked sound vibrations from a ship's propellers. The vibrations triggered a detonator (B) and exploded the mine.

To counter this weapon, Allied scientists developed an electrically-driven hammer. Placed in the bows of a merchant ship, it beat against the hull and made enough noise to detonate the mine well ahead. Minesweepers were equipped with a hammer box, a watertight case with a vibrating hammer inside, fitted in the bow.

The Germans also produced a combined magnetic-acoustic mine. These were cocked by the propeller noises of a passing ship, then magnetically exploded by the next ship passing over. This posed little problem for the minesweepers except that they had to make two sweeps of a suspected minefield. More dangerous was a later mine activated by the sudden change of water pressure as a ship passed over. No adequate counter-measure was developed.

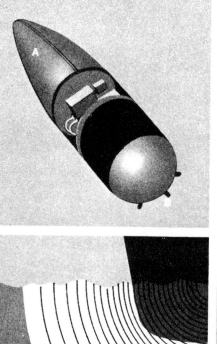

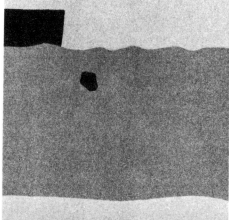

MINESWEEPING

Minesweeping was done by small shallow-draft vessels of wood or steel which were degaussed for protection against magnetic mines. They usually operated in pairs or several pairs but could also work on their own, as the one shown here clearing a field of moored contact mines. These mines were anchored to the seabed by sinker and cable, and lay just below the surface of the water, to explode when hit by a ship.

A minesweeper working on its own towed a steel cable which was suspended at the other end by an Oropesa float (A). The cable was kept at the required depth by an otter or kite (B), a steel frame in which planes were set like slanted steps in a ladder. The rush of water through the planes kept the towing cable down and away from the ship and maintained it in a long sweeping curve. Farther along the cable was a saw-toothed cutter (C). As the minesweeper moved through the water, its towing wire caught against the mine's mooring cable, drawing it down into the jaws of the cutter. Severed from its mooring, the contact mine floated to the surface where it was destroyed by rifle or machine-gun fire. When sweepers worked in pairs they towed a serrated cutting cable which was kept in position by two kites.

Magnetic minefields were cleared by an LL sweep (longitudinal sweep). Two mine-sweepers, equipped with generators and working abeam of each other, towed long buoyant electrical cables. Powerful pulses of electricity were passed down the cables. With the pulses synchronized, current flowed through the water between the cables, creating a magnetic field strong enough to trip the magnetic firing device and explode the mines well astern.

Ten vessels of the 31st Canadian Mine-sweeping Flotilla and six other Canadian minesweepers helped to clear the approaches to the Normandy invasion beaches early on D-Day. This sweep took them to within a mile and a half of the enemy coastal guns. The ships sailed on a set course and at a fixed speed in a tight overlapping formation (lower right) and with orders not to deviate from course no matter what opposition was met.

The leading sweeper trailed an Oropesa float on each side. Every other ship tucked herself behind the float of the sweeper ahead and so sailed through cleared water. To protect the leading sweeper, a shallow-draft Fairmile launch swept ahead, trailing its sweep across the leader's bow. As the sweepers advanced, dan buoys were dropped to mark the cleared channel. Shortly before dawn the job was done and the first assault craft of the invasion fleet came down the swept channel. The minesweepers had completely escaped the Germans' attention.

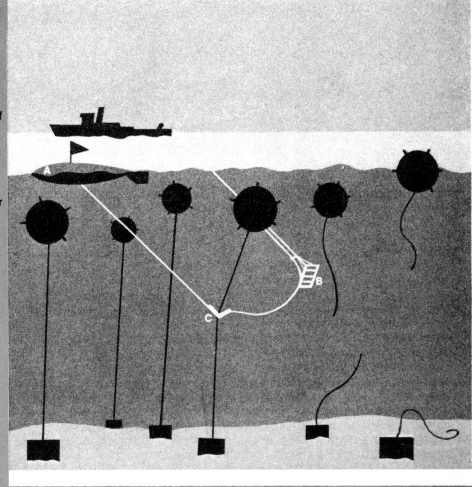

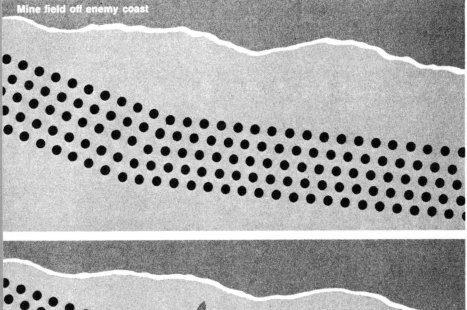

Mine field off enemy coast

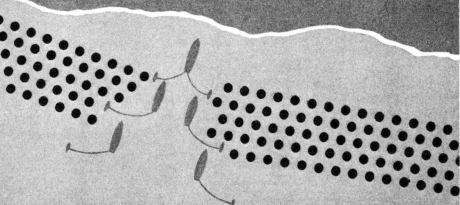

The infantryman walked with his free arm hanging slack, his other arm lolling snugly in the little hammock formed by his rifle sling and the butt of the rifle, his head tilted forward with the hint of a droop to it, his helmet set well back so that it rested on his head at the exact center of balance, and his feet gliding like slow pendulums, never more than an inch or two above the ground. His body did not rise or fall between steps, his arm did not swing, nor did his knees bend appreciably. The gait was the antithesis of marching; it was the soldier's gait as distinct from the military gait, the gait of men who had grown miserly of their energy, not through present weariness but through the knowledge of weariness to come. Most men never learned to walk like that until they had stumbled back from a battle half dead with exhaustion, cursing every betraying braggart muscle and swearing they'd never do so much as wiggle a finger again unless they could find a reason for it.

Ralph Allen in *Home Made Banners*

It was a shuffle and the only resemblance to marching was that they shuffled along in step. It ate up the miles with the least expenditure of energy. It was almost as if each soldier were praying: "Lord, you pick 'em up and I'll lay 'em down." Soldiers on campaign are always tired.

Maj. Gen. Chris Vokes

The War on Land

The Canadian infantryman of World War II was supported by a bewildering complexity of force and organization. Apart from the firepower of his own unit, there were planes to blast his battalion's objectives, tanks and flamethrowers which rumbled along beside him, artillery and heavy mortars and machine guns to take on difficult targets.

Behind the front were specialists who saw that food, ammunition and reinforcements went up, that the wounded were evacuated, that communications worked and that mail was delivered. Generals, brigadiers and colonels plotted the broad sweep of battle. Lieutenant colonels, majors, captains, lieutenants and sergeants worked out the more immediate tactics.

But ultimately everything pivoted on the infantryman himself, the individual human being with the courage God gave him and the weapons he could carry. The soldier with a rifle in his hands was still the classic figure of the front line.

An infantry division had three brigades and each brigade was made up of three battalions—units like the Queen's Own Rifles, the Black Watch, the Loyal Edmontons, the South Saskatchewans. There were as many as 850 men in a battalion; more than half —up to 500—were in four rifle companies. The infantry was the core of the army, the rifle companies the core of the infantry.

A rifle company—usually led by a major, with a captain second in command—was split into three platoons and each platoon into three sections. A platoon was commanded by a lieutenant backed by a sergeant; a section was led by a corporal.

Company weapons were rifles, light machine guns, grenades, submachine guns, light anti-tank weapons, light 2-inch mortars—things men could carry. Within its own battalion, a company could count on support from such weapons as 6-pounder anti-tank guns and 3-inch mortars.

On paper, a company had up to 125 men but it never had a full complement in action. There were always men sick, others away on leaves and courses, and men deliberately left out of battle (LOBs) to form a nucleus in the event of disaster. A company commander was doing well if he had 81 men, as Paul Triquet had when his company of the Royal 22nd Regiment assaulted Casa Berardi in Italy and he won the Victoria

Cross. If a company got below 50, it was in trouble because it could no longer do the job it was supposed to do.

Development of World War II weapons went back three decades. World War I had been a static war, a war of position. On the western front it ended almost where it began; the Allies won the last battle after repeated reverses and stalemate. Millions died and great areas were devastated but Germany was largely untouched. No foreign armies fought across German soil.

The Treaty of Versailles in 1919 cut German military strength to 100,000 men. But when Hitler came to power in 1933 a resurgence of militarism rebuilt Germany's general staff, her armies and her arsenal of weapons. German generals began a study of strategy (the overall aims of war and the broad means to achieve them) and of tactics (the employment of men and weapons on the battlefield). They developed a philosophy of movement combined with striking power.

The Allies held to the proven methods of the 1914-18 war—the war they'd won. They tended to ignore fresh ideas. French memories of 1.5 million war dead bred a defensive mentality and France built the Maginot Line. But it covered only part of the frontier with Germany; in the north, where German armies had poured into France in 1914, there were few defenses. Although France developed a formidable force of fine tanks, her generals looked on armor only as a support for infantry, not as a great tactical weapon in its own right. Britain experimented with armor but had only modest mobile formations.

Isolation and disenchantment with European politics led the United States to neglect her land forces. Of all the great powers in 1939, she had the least progressive military thinking and her weaponry was almost entirely of 1918 vintage.

From the outset, however, World War II bore scant similarity to 1918. It was a war of movement and supply. To strategy and tactics was added the science of logistics —provision of the means of war, where and when required, the planning of movement and the maintenance of forces.

In 1939 all evidence pointed to a conflict confined to Europe, but by the end of

1941 the war had become global. Logistics became the key to victory: how to maintain the effectiveness of an industrial base, the safety of lines of communication and a vast and complex inventory of weapons, fuel and equipment.

Seeking world domination, the Germans placed a high priority on shock power in mass. They developed *blitzkrieg* (lightning war) by using their army as a highly mobile force with great striking power. Armored fighting vehicles teamed with mechanized infantry (panzer grenadiers) and both worked closely with artillery and air support—and sometimes parachute troops. Blitzkrieg proved irresistible in Poland, the Low Countries and France. Later, in North Africa, this combination of infantry and armor with planes and big guns almost won Egypt and the Suez Canal. Germany's eventual defeat in Africa came as much from failure of logistics as from the great British offensive which started at El Alamein.

To counter blitzkrieg, the Allies turned infantry battalions into virtual small armies, each with its own machine guns, transport, anti-tank weapons and artillery (in the form of mortars). Tracked and half-tracked vehicles increased infantry mobility and specialist battalions were dropped by parachute or carried into battle by gliders and transport planes.

These advances led to development of new personal and crew-manned weapons to increase infantry firepower. While the 1914-18 soldier had to rely mainly on aimed rifle fire, World War II saw a proliferation of automatic arms classed as submachine guns and light and heavy machine guns. Mortars, for hitting obscured targets by firing shells at high angles, were lightened and their ammunition improved. Anti-tank weapons were improved.

The Germans, meanwhile, added light artillery to their infantry battalions, as well as rockets fired from the 150-mm. Nebelwerfer, a 6-barrel launcher called the Moaning Minnie.

Light Weapons

In 1939 Canada armed her soldiers with World War I weapons: the Webley .455 pistol and the short-magazine No. 1 Lee

Enfield rifle. The army had a few Bren .303 light machine guns. The Boys .55 anti-tank rifle was the only weapon of its type and there were few of them. Local defenses and training establishments—and the first formations to go overseas—used the .303 Lewis and .303 Vickers machine guns.

In time, Canada achieved wonders for a nation that had no prewar munitions industry. Large numbers of the Bren light machine gun and Boys anti-tank rifle were produced from 1940 on. By November 1942, overseas units received the first No. 4 Lee Enfields, from British production; from June 1943 on this issue rifle came from a government arsenal at Long Branch, Ont. The Webley pistol was replaced during the war by the Canadian 9-mm. Browning automatic.

The famous Sten submachine gun made its debut in 1942. It fired 9-mm. ammunition, the kind used in the German Luger pistol and standard in many European countries. The Sten was produced at a cost of $9. Its only drawback was a tendency to fire prematurely if handled roughly.

The inadequacy of the Boys anti-tank rifle against improved armor spurred production of the British-designed PIAT (Projector Infantry Anti-Tank). It came into service in 1942. This shoulder-fired weapon launched a rocket that was extremely effective against armor, pillboxes and vehicles at close range.

An adaptation of the Universal (Bren) Carrier to mount a flamethrower was a joint Anglo-Canadian project. The first version, the Ronson, was succeeded by the Wasp, manufactured in Canada.

German light weapons were first-class in design and construction. The 9-mm. Luger pistol, the official German side arm since 1908, was a semi-automatic, recoil-operated weapon with a toggle-joint bolt action. It was superseded during the war by the Walther P38, also 9-mm.

The German issue rifle was a shortened and otherwise improved version of a Mauser which went back to 1908—a weapon whose longevity in service equaled that of the British Lee Enfield rifle. The Mauser, a bolt-operated magazine-fed carbine of 7.92-mm. caliber, was equipped with a 10-inch knife bayonet and had an effective range of 800 yards.

The Treaty of Versailles had imposed rigid limitations on arms manufacture in Germany. What design and development did take place had to be done in secret by German-owned firms in other countries. But

when Hitler repudiated the treaty, production of automatic arms moved swiftly ahead. The MP38 submachine gun, developed in 1936 and used by police and border patrols, was adopted by the army, primarily for paratroop and armored units. The improved MP40 went into service in 1940. Both were 9-mm. weapons fed by 32-round box-magazines.

Late in the war Germany introduced a 7.92-mm. assault rifle, a weapon intended to replace rifle, submachine gun and light machine gun. Some assault rifles were issued in 1944 to paratroopers operating as ground troops, but this weapon came too late to be of great significance.

Germany made outstanding progress with light machine guns. The versatile Mauser

MG34, which went into service in 1938, could be fired from a bipod, from a tripod with an adapter and special sight or from a special mount as an anti-aircraft gun. It was mounted in many types of vehicles and aircraft and was the mainstay of the rifle squad; the riflemen's first task was to support and protect the two-man MG34 crew. The remarkable MG42, designed for cheap mass production and introduced in 1942, fired more than 1000 rounds a minute. Long after the war it was still rated the best of its type in the world.

Enemy infantry was well equipped with mortars. At platoon level the Germans used a 50-mm. mortar firing a 2.2-pound high-explosive shell with a top range of 570 yards. The heavy weapons company also had six 81-mm. mortars which lifted 7.75-pound high-explosive shells up to 2600

yards. This weapon was later replaced by 120-mm. mortar to counter a Russia weapon of similar caliber.

The most common German grenade wa the Stielhandgranate 24, a stick grenad known as a potato masher. Another was th egg-shaped Eierhandgranate 39. These mis siles, normally thrown, were also set a booby traps or demolition charges.

Two other light infantry weapons wer the Panzerfaust, a recoilless anti-tank gre nade fired from a launching tube, and a 88-mm. 7-pound projectile called the Pan zerschreck (tank terror). Each was shoul der-fired by one man.

Tanks

Few advances in ground warfare in Worl War II were as startling as the developmen of armored fighting vehicles.

The western powers tended at first to divide tanks into two types. The lightl armed but fast and mobile cruiser tank wa intended to scout and probe as cavalry ha done. The slower but heavily armored infantry tank was to give direct support to assaulting infantry by overcoming machin guns and fixed defenses. But experience showed the need for a medium tank like the Sherman M4, which was capable o doing both jobs if used in large enough num bers. Canadian armored units used the Sherman and, for reconnaissance, the Stuar M3 light tank, known as the Honey.

Most of the German tanks in the invasion of Poland were lightly armed and armored Not until May 1940 did German armo meet significant opposition, chiefly from

Britain's new Matilda tanks. Although armed with only a 2-pounder (40-mm.) gun, the Matilda had armor twice as thick as the German tank armor.

France had 3000 well-armed modern tanks but used them piecemeal, not as one massive and potentially decisive weapon.

The Germans revolutionized tank design when they found their Panzer IV was no match for the Russian T34 medium tank they encountered on the eastern front in 1941. The T34 had all the qualities of a great fighting tank—a big gun (76-mm.), speed (up to 33 m.p.h.), mobility, firepower and excellent well-sloped protective armor. To try to match the T34, the Germans gave the Panzer IV a long 75-mm. gun and developed self-propelled anti-tank guns. But the real answers were Germany's new heavy battle tanks, the Panther and

Tiger. The Panther went into action in 1943. With its 4.3-inch turret armor and long-barreled, high-velocity 75-mm. gun, it outmatched the T34. The 76-ton Tiger II, armed with the famous 88-mm. gun, overwhelmed all opposition.

Impressive advances were made in the hitting power of projectiles fired from tank-mounted and anti-tank guns. In 1939, simple armor-piercing shot and some high-explosive shells could penetrate light armor. But as thicker plate was introduced to cope with high-velocity guns, new techniques were sought. One improvement was the discarding sabot round: the hard core of the projectile was cased in a wrapping that squeezed the shot as it passed through the barrel, then fell clear, imparting greater velocity to the core. Another was the hollow-charge, high-explosive anti-tank round: the low-velocity shell detonated against enemy armor, then directed a stream of high-velocity molten debris which punched a hole through the hull. The same principle was applied to hand-held weapons such as the American Bazooka, the PIAT and the German Panzerfaust.

A single Sherman M4—this tank was standard in all Allied forces—had virtually no chance against a Panther or Tiger. But the Firefly, a Sherman mounting the long 17-pounder (76.2-mm.) instead of the 75-mm. gun, could handle a Panther and was almost equal to a Tiger and its 88.

It was Allied quantity that defeated German quality. Commanders frequently risked three 75-mm. Shermans to destroy one Panther or Tiger—and the cost was frequently two of the three.

There were tanks for specialized functions—the Funnies of Maj. Gen. Sir Percy Hobart's 79th British Armored Division. Its Churchill Armored Vehicle Royal Artillery (AVRE) mounted a mortar which fired a 40-pound concrete-buster called a Flying Dustbin. The AVRE could also carry boughs for filling in ditches and craters so tanks could cross. The Churchill Crocodile was fitted as a flamethrower, towing a trailer containing 400 gallons of fuel. Another of the Funnies carried a small box girder bridge for crossing seawalls and anti-tank ditches. One weird Churchill variant was the Snake. It carried long pipes filled with high explosive; they could be joined and pushed across a mined area and exploded, detonating the mines.

Another brilliant modification of a conventional tank was the swimming or Duplex Drive (DD) Sherman M4. Launched

from landing craft, DDs ran for the Normandy beaches under their own power. Not all made it in the choppy seas of June 6, 1944, but those that did gave tremendous fire support to the infantry.

A purely Canadian development was the Kangaroo, an armored personnel carrier designed to protect infantry accompanying tanks across fireswept ground. The Canadian-built Ram II tank and the Priest self-propelled gun carriage were converted for this purpose. In each case the gun was removed.

Artillery

Six years of war bred marked changes in conventional artillery. In World War I, mobility had not been of primary importance and many effective if unwieldy weapons did yeoman service. By 1939 all towed artillery in the British and Canadian forces was mechanized. Most German guns were horse-drawn until after the invasion of Russia in 1941; then the urgency of mobility, speed and cross-country capability placed the emphasis on self-propelled guns.

Britain entered the war with two excellent designs for field and medium artillery, and both were adopted by Canada.

The first was the 25-pounder gun howitzer, capable of firing at a high angle at unseen targets or, in an anti-tank role, of firing armor-piercing ammunition with a flat trajectory. Its normal range was 12,500 yards and it was towed by a tractor known as a quad. The Canadians later designed and built a self-propelled version called the Sexton, a 25-pounder mounted on a Ram tank chassis. It came into service in 1943.

The second weapon was the 5.5-inch medium gun/howitzer which fired an 82-pound high-explosive shell up to 18,000 yards. It was towed by a 5-ton tractor.

For anti-tank defenses, the Canadians started with the 2-pounder gun on a field carriage. It was followed by the 6-pounder and in 1944 by the 17-pounder.

World War II saw great advances in anti-aircraft artillery. The British, Canadians and Americans employed the 40-mm. Bofors on a field carriage as a light anti-aircraft weapon. A British heavy ack-ack gun was the 3.7-inch, an excellent gun also used in the field. The 4.5- and 5.25-inch anti-aircraft guns were restricted to fixed installations defending vital areas.

The German Army went to war with a wide array of guns. Infantry regiments used the 37-mm. anti-tank gun, the 75-mm. howitzer and the 150-mm. heavy infantry howitzer. Except for the 150-mm., these were light, easily handled, close-support weapons. In 1941 a heavier anti-tank gun, the 50-mm. Pak 38, was introduced.

The German equivalent of the British 25-pounder field artillery piece was the 105-mm. gun/howitzer, which was modified into several self-propelled versions. As a result of battle experience, it was given a more flexible mounting, a heavier charge and a long-range shell. Experience in Russia had taught the Germans that all guns must have an anti-tank capability as well as all-round traverse.

The celebrated German 88-mm. flak gun, designed in the late 1920s, was issued to units in 1933 and battle-tested in the Spanish civil war. It went through several modifications until the Flak 41 came into service in 1943. The 88's abilities as an anti-tank weapon were devastatingly demonstrated by Rommel in North Africa. Mounted in tanks, tank-destroyers and coastal defense emplacements, the 88 earned a fearsome reputation as an anti-personnel weapon as well. Canadian troops spoke of it with awe.

The big powers began the war with strong cadres of professional soldiers.

The prewar British Army had broad experience in many climates and was outstanding in discipline, fieldcraft and weapons training. Restricted by the Treaty of Versailles, the men who built Germany's prewar army enlisted only the best recruits and strove for quality. Training covered all arms and every type of weapon. Every soldier was schooled to be a leader.

The Canadian Army in 1939 had a tiny Permanent Force and a semi-trained militia but, essentially, it had to start from scratch. It learned quickly and received long, intensive training before being committed to battle. It was even said Canadian troops were over-trained. But the endless exercises and rehearsals—and the bloody raid on Dieppe in 1942—paid off in relatively light casualties on D-Day in Normandy. Throughout the war, Canadians developed a professional attitude toward soldiering. There was scope for initiative and original thinking, as shown by the adoption of improvisations such as the Sexton and Kangaroo and the tactics for their employment.

All armies had to learn to meld their infantry, armor, artillery, assault engineers and airpower into combat groups. The German Army did this in early campaigns but

strained relations with the Luftwaffe eventually led to problems. Army commanders were even denied the use of Luftwaffe guns they needed for anti-tank work.

In Commonwealth armies, including the Canadian Army, cooperation steadily improved until air support of ground operations became routine. This helped maintain morale, the core of an offensive military spirit. The military hierarchy was deeply conscious that there must be no repetition of World War I's senseless waste of human lives; the soldiers had confidence they

would not be needlessly sacrificed. Technology helped make this possible by providing machines to replace flesh and blood.

But probably nothing contributed more to morale than efficient medical services in the field, backed by rapid evacuation to hospitals. Many lives were saved that would not have been saved in previous wars. There were improvements in field rations and in the amenities that made a combat soldier's life more bearable. There was none of the agony and demoralization of the trench warfare of 1914-18, although conditions in Italy and Holland at times came close to it.

It was a different war in many ways, but some things did not change. One constant in all warfare is that success and ultimate victory depend on the stamina and courage of the individual soldier, combined with good leadership. As his father had done in World War I, the Canadian soldier proved himself a first-class fighting man, lacking neither initiative nor courage.

AN INFANTRY BATTALION ATTACKS

No two infantry assaults were the same but this illustration indicates how an attack might be made by a battalion of 850 men. They are supported by a squadron of 16 tanks, 12 six-pounder anti-tank guns (in addition to six in the battalion's own anti-tank platoon), four 17-pounders and eight 25-pounders.

With each leading company (A and B) is an artillery forward observation officer who feeds target information to the guns. Each forward company is supported by four tanks and each has two platoons forward and one in reserve with company HQ. (Each platoon has in it a pistol, rifles, Sten or Thompson submachine guns, three Brens, a 2-inch mortar and a PIAT

(Projectile, Infantry, Anti-Tank). PIATs are also carried by the battalion's 3-inch mortar and anti-tank platoons and by company HQ.)

Each forward company is supported by two 6-pounders. Heavy machine guns (.303 Vickers) are on the flanks. They and the 4.2-inch mortars belong to the divisional machine-gun battalion. These mortars and the infantry battalion's own 3-inch mortars are near the battalion's tactical headquarters. Farther back are the 12 remaining 6-pounders and a troop of 17-pounders, all from the divisional anti-tank regiment, and a battery of divisional 25-pounders.

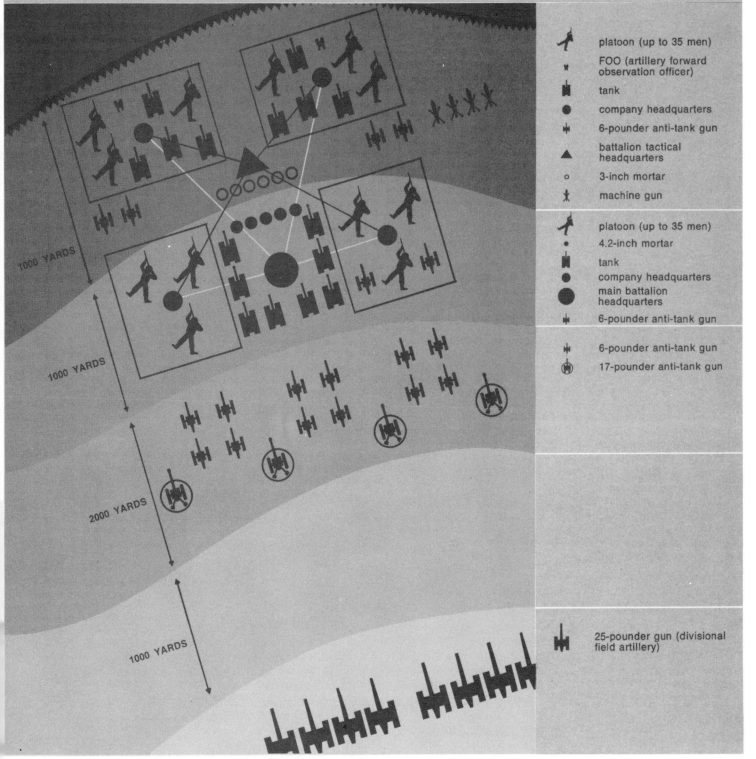

platoon (up to 35 men)	
FOO (artillery forward observation officer)	
tank	
company headquarters	
6-pounder anti-tank gun	
battalion tactical headquarters	
3-inch mortar	
machine gun	
platoon (up to 35 men)	
4.2-inch mortar	
tank	
company headquarters	
main battalion headquarters	
6-pounder anti-tank gun	
6-pounder anti-tank gun	
17-pounder anti-tank gun	
25-pounder gun (divisional field artillery)	

1000 YARDS

1000 YARDS

2000 YARDS

1000 YARDS

TYPE 36 GRENADE

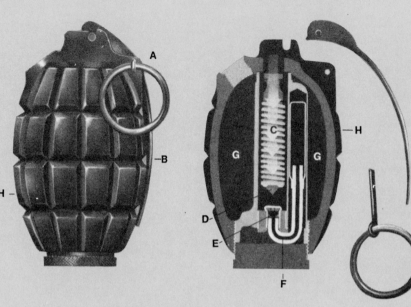

The grenade was the smallest but one of the most important of infantry weapons, a simple bomb used with great effect in assaults on pillboxes, machine-gun nests and small concentrations of troops. Once the firing pin is pulled, nothing can deactivate a grenade and it explodes whether it hits its target or not.

Grenades were first used as weapons of war in the 15th century. The earliest versions were thrown by hand and measured about 3¼ inches in diameter. They were shaped like pomegranates—and that's how they got their name. Early types were apt to burst prematurely and only men of considerable skill and courage were picked to use them. During the 17th century European armies began to field grenadier units and they became elite troops.

In World War I the British produced the No. 5 or Mills pattern grenade, fitted with a time fuse that was not ignited until the bomb left the hand. The weapon's effective range depended upon the throwing ability of the user. Modified for use with a cup discharger, it became the Type 36 and could be either thrown by hand in close combat, in the traditional manner, or fired from a rifle. The 36 was widely used by Canadian and other Allied troops in World War II.

The grenade is filled with high explosive and detonated by a fuse ignited by a cartridge,cap. When the safety pin (A) is removed, the striker lever (B) is kept in place by the soldier's grip until he throws the grenade. As the lever is released, the striker spring (C) forces the striker down and the striker head (D) hits the cartridge cap (E). After a delay of four to five seconds—as the grenade is in the air on its way to the target and the fuse (F) burns—the high explosive (G) is touched off. The case (H) breaks into as many as 80 pieces, producing a lethal shrapnel effect.

STIELHANDGRANATE 24

German grenades were designed for blast effect and were considered "offensive" weapons as opposed to "defensive" types such as the Type 36 with its fragmentation. This *Stielhandgranate* (stick hand grenade) was nicknamed the potato masher. It had a thin iron or steel casing or head (A) filled with explosive and containing a detonator. The head was screwed into a hollow wooden handle (B). In the handle was a cord—one end attached to a lead ball which was part of a friction-igniter-detonator system, the other attached to a small porcelain ball stowed in a cavity at the base of the handle. Over this cavity was a screw-on metal cap (C). In action, the cap was removed, the porcelain ball was pulled out as far as it would go, and the grenade was thrown. The fuse gave a four- or five-second delay before explosion. The blast radius was 12 to 14 yards. Potato mashers were carried in pocketed sleeveless jackets or stuck in belts or jackboots.

LEE ENFIELD RIFLE, NO. 4, MARK I*

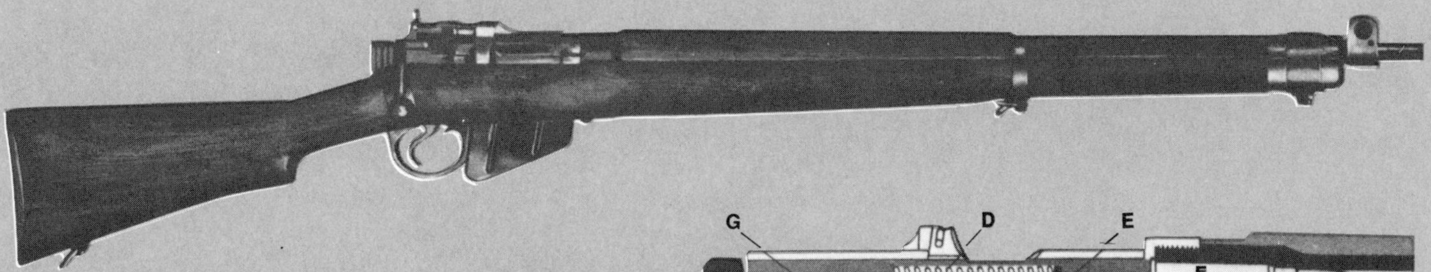

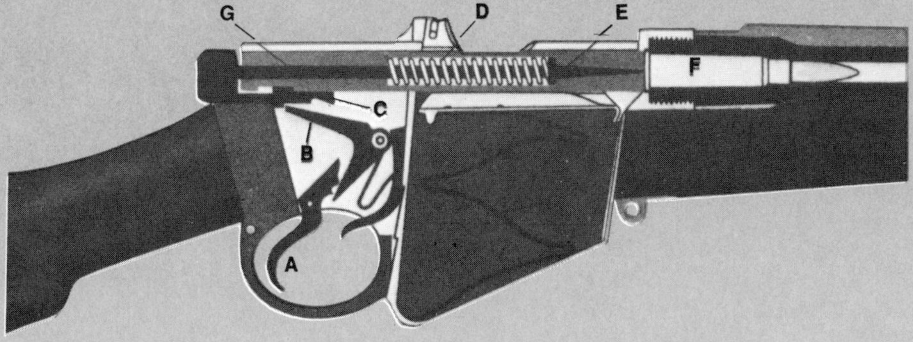

The simple bolt-action rifle was probably *the* standard weapon of the war. Canadian infantrymen used it wherever they fought. Their rifle was the British Lee Enfield whose basic design dated from the 1890s. Until November 1942—after Hong Kong and Dieppe but before Sicily—they carried the Short Magazine Lee Enfield No. 1, a refinement of the rifle their fathers had used in World War I. Then the No. 4 was issued and in June 1943 the Canadians started using No. 4s made in Canada and designated the Mark I*. Its box-type magazine, extending through the bottom of the stock forward of the trigger guard, carried two 5-round clips of .303 ammunition. A trained soldier could fire the 10 rounds in slightly less than a minute and be effective up to 900 yards. Shorter ranges, up to 600 yards, were more common. The Lee Enfield was the fastest-operating bolt-action rifle in the world. It could also launch a grenade from a cup adapter or discharger.

The cutaway illustration shows the rifle at the moment of firing. With the pulling of the trigger (A), the sear (B) has been disengaged from the full bent (C) and the striker spring (D) is released. The striker (E) hits the round (F) in the chamber. Now the rifle can be cocked again. As the bolt (G) is pulled back and the striker spring (D) is compressed, another round will be forced up into the chamber by the magazine spring (H).

Canada manufactured almost a million Lee Enfields during the war. Various sights could be fitted. A superior locking system and easy field maintenance helped make the Lee Enfield superior to most other bolt-action rifles.

MAUSER KAR 98K

The standard infantry weapon of the German Army in World War II was the Mauser Kar 98K. Kar is for *Karbiner* (carbine or short rifle) and K stands for *Kurz* (short). This weapon therefore was a shortened version of the original Kar 98 which was taken into service in 1908. The Kar 98K was a bolt-operated rifle firing 7.92-mm. (.312-inch) ammunition in 5-round clips. The effective range was 800 yards but a maximum of about 3000 was possible. Sighting was by an inverted V blade front sight and leaf type at the rear. The Mauser was loaded in the same manner as the Lee Enfield, the empty clip being ejected as the bolt was closed and a new round being forced into the chamber from the magazine. A short knife bayonet was made for the Kar 98K and it could be fitted with any of several types of rifle grenade launchers.

THOMPSON .45 SUBMACHINE GUN

Submachine guns came into their own in World War II. Light like rifles, fast like machine guns, they were popular with all armies. The Finns used them with devastating effect against the Russians in 1939-40. Later, the Russians used them in great numbers in their battles with the Germans. Allied armies found submachine guns invaluable for special purposes such as commando and paratroop attacks and to bolster rifle fire. The Canadians stocked the American Thompson—the famous tommy gun or "Chicago piano" of the prewar prohibition era—and the Sten. The Thompson could fire at a rate of 650 rounds a minute, feeding from a box or drum magazine. Like all submachine guns it was less accurate than a rifle and had a short range. The cutaway illustration shows its operation. As the trigger (A) is pressed, the sear (B) disengages from the bolt (C). The compressed recoil spring (D) reasserts itself, driving the bolt forward.

The face of the bolt strikes the base of the next cartridge in the magazine (E), carrying it into the chamber. The extractor (F) springs into the grooved base of the cartridge. Just before the bolt reaches its forward position, the bottom forward end of the triangular hammer (G) strikes the receiver. The hammer pivots around the hammer pin (H). The upper part strikes the head of the firing pin (I), firing the cartridge.

SCHMEISSER MP38

The Schmeisser was tops among German *Maschinenpistolen* (submachine guns) and outstanding for close combat and street fighting. It was issued to infantry platoon and section commanders and to tank and armored-vehicle crews. The design was excellent—a simple blowback (recoil) operation—but the weapon was expensive to produce. It used 9-mm. ammunition, had a 32-round magazine and was effective to 200 yards. With loaded magazine, the Schmeisser weighed 9½ pounds.

STEN 9-mm. SUBMACHINE GUN

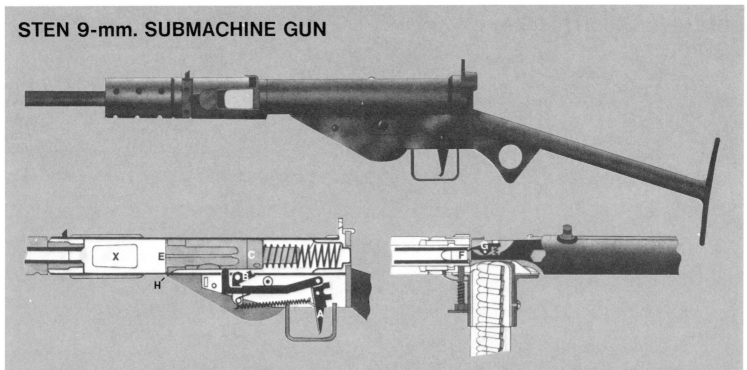

In 1939 the British had no submachine gun. After the fall of France in 1940 they realized the need to develop one that could be mass-produced cheaply. The answer was the Sten, its name a combination of the initials of its designers, Sheppherd and Turpin, with the first two letters of Enfield, the British arsenal. The Sten was simplicity itself; it had only 47 parts, most of them stamped from metal like cookies formed by a cutter, and they were welded, sweated or riveted together. It was so simple that Resistance groups in Europe could make it for themselves. It had still another advantage: it used 9-mm. ammunition and lots of it was captured from the Germans. With its 32-round magazine in place on the left of the gun, at right angles to the barrel (in hole X above), the Sten weighed only 9½ pounds. It could be fired in automatic bursts or in single shots and its range was 200 yards. The Canadians first used the Sten at Dieppe. It had its detractors at first but good training soon convinced most soldiers of its

virtues. The cutaway illustrations show the Sten from the side (left cutaway) and from above (right cutaway—note magazine in place). With the pulling of the trigger (A), the sear (B) is disengaged from the breech block (C) and the return spring (D) drives the firing pin (E) against the round (F). Gas pressure created by the firing of the cartridge forces the breech block to the rear, compressing the return spring. As the breech block travels to the rear, the extractor (G)— already engaged in the groove of the cartridge case— extracts the case from the chamber and it is ejected out the right side of the gun. As the breech block bent (H) rides over the sear (B), the sear is forced down and engages in front of the bent, holding the breech block to the rear and readying the gun to fire another round. The Sten was fitted with a fixed aperture sight set for 100 yards. The gun could be used with a silencer—a particularly good feature in commando operations.

STURMGEWEHR MP44

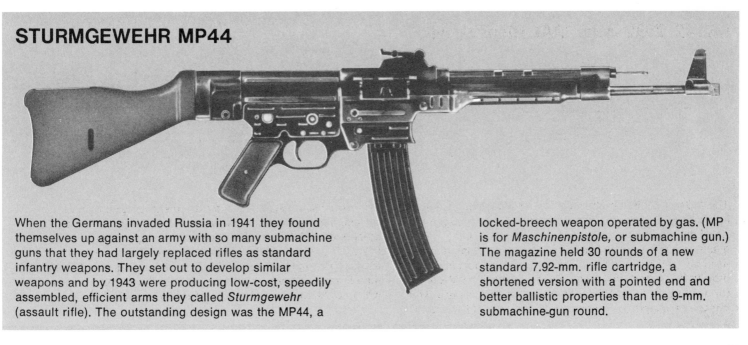

When the Germans invaded Russia in 1941 they found themselves up against an army with so many submachine guns that they had largely replaced rifles as standard infantry weapons. They set out to develop similar weapons and by 1943 were producing low-cost, speedily assembled, efficient arms they called *Sturmgewehr* (assault rifle). The outstanding design was the MP44, a

locked-breech weapon operated by gas. (MP is for *Maschinenpistole*, or submachine gun.) The magazine held 30 rounds of a new standard 7.92-mm. rifle cartridge, a shortened version with a pointed end and better ballistic properties than the 9-mm. submachine-gun round.

BREN .303 LIGHT MACHINE GUN

The Bren, a basic infantry weapon and one of the finest light machine guns ever made, originated in Czechoslovakia as the Brno ZB and was adopted by Britain in 1932. The British improved it, modified it to take .303 rifle ammunition and called it the Bren, a combination of Brno and Enfield, the British arsenal. Canada made many thousands of these air-cooled, gas-operated weapons. The Bren weighed 22 pounds and had a two-man crew but was fired by one man from a bipod or even at the hip. The normal rate of fire from a 30-round magazine was five bursts of four or five rounds a minute. The effective range was 500 yards. A very fast operator could deliver 150 rounds a minute; on full automatic it could get off 500. The Bren could be converted into a heavy machine gun, firing from a solid tripod mount, or into an anti-aircraft gun. It was also used on vehicles. The cutaway illustration shows the Bren immediately after firing. Gas behind the bullet escapes from the barrel through a gas regulator (A) to operate the piston (B) and make the weapon ready for further firing. At this same split second the spent cartridge (C) will be ejected and a new round forced down from the spring-loaded magazine (D). The barrel had to be changed after firing three or four magazines; a red hot barrel could be plunged into cold water without damaging the metal.

MG42 7.92-mm. MACHINE GUN

The MG42 (MG is the abbreviation for *Maschinengewehr,* machine gun) was considered the outstanding weapon of the war. Like the Bren, it was a multi-purpose gun: light machine gun on a bipod (as here), heavy machine gun on a tripod, and anti-aircraft weapon. Designed for mass production, it had one great advantage over the MG34 (opposite page) apart from improved performance: it was cheap and simple to make. Its very high rate of fire—up to 1200 rounds a minute—could be a disadvantage except against planes. Ammunition was fed into it from 50-round steel belts which could be linked into multiples. Alternatively it fed off a 75-round double-saddle type of magazine, actually two magazines combined and sending rounds into the chamber alternately. With its bipod, the MG42 weighed 26 pounds. Its effective range was 600 yards.

VICKERS .303 MACHINE GUN MARK 1

Canadians used the Vickers .303 machine gun in both world wars and it wasn't finally retired until 1968, some 85 years after the first patents were taken out. It was fathered by an American, Hiram Maxim, a self-taught engineering genius. Britain acquired rights to produce the gun he designed and when the Maxim patents expired it was called the Vickers gun, after Albert Vickers, its manufacturer. Classed as a medium weapon, the Vickers could be fired at high or low angles, from a tripod, as here. It operated on a simple gas-assisted recoil system, was water-cooled and was fed by belts of .303 ammunition. Its accurate range was 1100 yards but it could reach much farther.

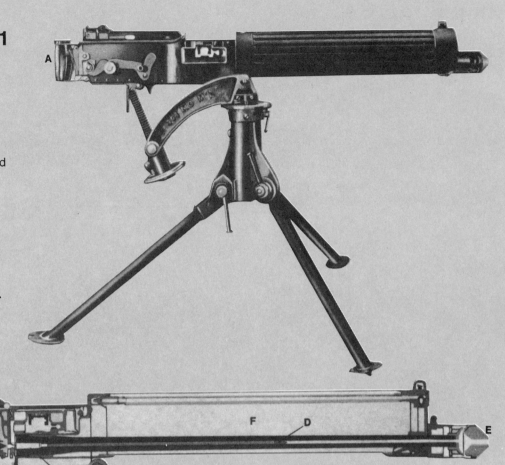

The Vickers fired in full automatic bursts of 10 to 20 rounds; 60 shots a minute rated as slow fire, 250 as rapid fire. In addition to ground warfare, it was used in aircraft and as an anti-aircraft weapon. The gun's two traversing handles—one is shown (A) in each of these illustrations—are grasped by the man firing the weapon. With both thumbs he presses the trigger (B). Now the gun will fire as long as the trigger is kept pushed in and cartridges are fed into the breech. As the cartridge (C) explodes, the bullet (D) is driven down the barrel and the locked barrel and locking mechanism start rearward. When the bullet leaves the barrel, gases behind it expand in the muzzle attachment (E) and help the recoil action. Water (F) around the barrel keeps the gun from overheating. It is circulated by hose from a container alongside.

7.92-mm. MG34

The Treaty of Versailles banned German manufacture of heavy machine guns after World War I. The Germans got around that by designing the MG34 as an all-purpose gun using their standard 7.92-mm. service cartridge. It was classified as a light machine gun and, in the war, was widely used by all German armed forces. Mounted on a bipod, it was used as a light machine gun with a range of up to 2000 yards. On a tripod, as here, it nearly doubled its range as a heavy machine gun and anti-aircraft weapon. It could fire up to 900 rounds a minute and was normally fed by a metal link belt of ammunition. Like the Vickers, it was a recoil-operated, gas-assisted weapon but was air-cooled.

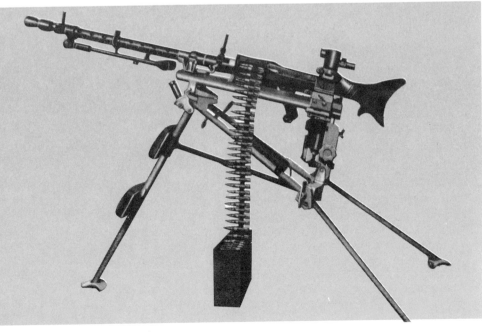

3-INCH MORTAR

Mortars were designed to beef up an infantry battalion's firepower by lobbing shells into enemy positions from a high angle. This 3-inch, the standard heavy infantry mortar, was the main weapon of a battalion's support company and could hit targets as close as 125 yards or as distant as 2800. A crew of three transported it in a Universal Carrier and manhandled it in three parts: the smooth-bore barrel (A), the mounting (B) which in action supported the barrel and provided elevating and transversing adjustments, and the base plate (C) which absorbed the shock of firing. Once the mortar was set up, a 10-pound bomb was dropped down the barrel (cutaway, right) and hit a striker stud (D) which fired a propellant cartridge (E) in the tail of the bomb. When the bomb landed, a striker (F) set off its explosive (G).

The mortar projected three types of bomb: smoke (H), high explosive (I) or star (J). The tail unit was fitted with six vanes to which augmenting charges could be attached to increase the range of the weapon. Mortars, like most weapons, were scarce at the start: in the spring of 1939 the army received *five* from Britain—when every battalion was supposed to have two. Eventually the army used three types: the 4.2-inch, firing a 20-pound bomb; the 3-inch with its 10-pound bomb, and the 2-inch, an infantry platoon weapon using a 2½-pound bomb.

80-mm. HEAVY MORTAR

This was the standard German infantry mortar, similar to the 3-inch mortar the Canadians used. It also broke down into three parts and was fired in the same way. A smooth-bore, muzzle-loading weapon, it could fire high-explosive or smoke shells to a minimum range of 66 yards or a maximum of 2078. Served by a three-man crew, it was fired by dropping the bomb into the barrel tail first. When the bomb struck a fixed firing pin, the propellant charge (similar to a 12-gauge shotgun shell) was detonated and the projectile unleashed. The Germans were masterful in their use of mortars and this one was a redoubtable foe of the Canadians in Italy and western Europe. In action a German mortar crew normally carried 24 shells.

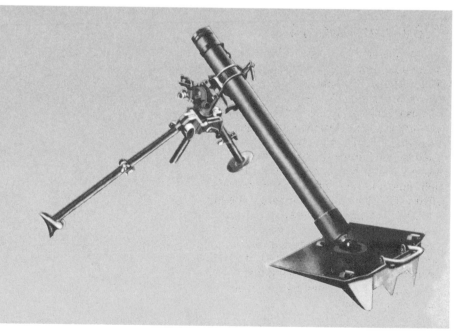

PIAT (PROJECTOR, INFANTRY, ANTI-TANK)

Pte. Ernest "Smoky" Smith used a PIAT on the night in October 1944 when he broke up a series of German counter-attacks and won the Victoria Cross in a bridgehead over the Savio River in Italy. It was never a popular weapon; it had a considerable recoil and a soldier had to take it to within 100 yards of a tank to be very effective. In full view of the enemy, Smith stopped a Panther with a single bomb at 10 yards! Experts consider the PIAT probably the most unusual standard-issue weapon employed by Commonwealth forces. The 32-pound launcher (right), which fired a 2½-pound bomb (below, right), was a kind of cross between an anti-tank rifle and a bazooka. It was simple in design and construction and to operate it required no elaborate training. It was effective against all German tanks if accurately fired at the side armor.

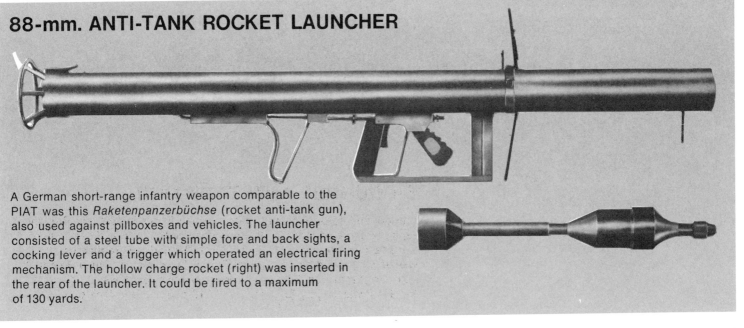

Operation of the PIAT was simple. The bomb, tail tube (A) first, was slid onto a spigot inside the launcher. When the trigger (B) was pulled, it released the spigot on a powerful spring, driving it forward. A firing pin in the head of the spigot struck and detonated a propellant cartridge (C). This explosion fired the bomb, with its shaped hollow charge of high explosive (D), and drove the spigot back, cocking it for another shot. Also shown are the shoulder piece (E) with shoulder pad and laced cover, backsight (F) and foresight (G), safety catch lever (H), trigger assembly and grip (I) and front support (J). "Although the weapon is fired from the shoulder," said an army manual, "the action on firing is very different from that of a rifle or machine gun. When the trigger action has released the spigot, a total weight of about 12 pounds travels forward for one tenth of a second before the round is fired. The backward thrust on the shoulder is increased and the balance of the weapon changes slightly. The aim has to be kept steady against these effects."

88-mm. ANTI-TANK ROCKET LAUNCHER

A German short-range infantry weapon comparable to the PIAT was this *Raketenpanzerbüchse* (rocket anti-tank gun), also used against pillboxes and vehicles. The launcher consisted of a steel tube with simple fore and back sights, a cocking lever and a trigger which operated an electrical firing mechanism. The hollow charge rocket (right) was inserted in the rear of the launcher. It could be fired to a maximum of 130 yards.

25-POUNDER GUN/HOWITZER

The 25-pounder was the workhorse of Commonwealth field artillery units.
A six-man crew could get it into action in about one minute—either as
a gun, firing armor-piercing shells with a flat trajectory, or as a
howitzer, firing high-explosive shells at a high angle. The gun was
effective up to 12,500 yards; with a supercharge, up to 13,400. From
July 1941 this fine weapon was manufactured in Canada.

6-POUNDER ANTI-TANK GUN

Introduced into British and Commonwealth forces in 1941, the 6-pounder
replaced the 2-pounder in 1942 and became the main anti-tank gun of
Canada's infantry units. It was also used by anti-tank regiments. It
was usually towed by a Universal Carrier but sometimes by a Ram tank
with turret removed. The 6-pounder's effective range was 1000 yards.
In 1944 it was largely replaced by the 17-pounder anti-tank gun.

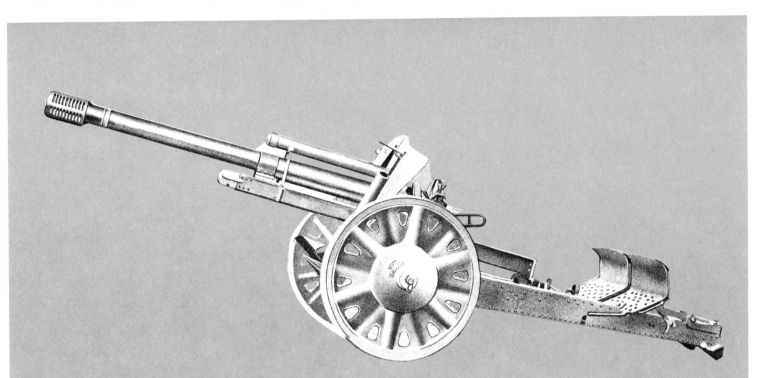

105-mm. GUN / HOWITZER

Roughly the equivalent of the Anglo-Canadian 25-pounder, this was the standard weapon of the German divisional field artillery. It fired high-explosive, star, smoke and incendiary shells—and propaganda leaflets—to a maximum of 13,480 yards. Like all gun/howitzers, it could be fired at low or high angles. This model (F18) dates back to World War I; an improved model, the F18/40, was introduced in 1944.

50-mm. PAK 38

The German Army started the war with a 37-mm. anti-tank gun which proved ineffective against most tank armor. In 1941 they replaced it with this 50-mm. (1.97-inch) Pak 38, which had a crew of eight and was normally towed by a half-track. It fired armor-piercing shells to 880 yards, high-explosive shells to 2000. Mounted on a single axle with two rubber-tired wheels, it had a conventional split-trail carriage.

5.5-INCH GUN/HOWITZER

Designed and put into production shortly before the war, the 5.5-inch gun-howitzer was used by the Canadians as a medium artillery weapon. It replaced the obsolete 6-inch howitzers of World War I vintage. Mounted on a two-wheel carriage, the 5.5 fired an 82-pound high-explosive projectile up to 18,200 yards—nearly 11 miles—at two rounds a minute. It was handled by a 10-man crew and was transported by a five-ton tractor known as a Matador.

3.7-INCH ANTI-AIRCRAFT GUN

When Churchill and Roosevelt went to Quebec City for wartime conferences, the city was protected by 3.7-inch guns, the standard heavy anti-aircraft weapons in British service. The 3.7 was as good a gun as Germany's great multi-purpose 88-mm. but it never achieved the same reputation, partly because its potential as an anti-tank weapon was not fully developed. Its maximum effective range was 32,000 feet.

88-mm. FLAK 41

No German weapon was held in greater awe by Allied fighting men—and none provoked more profanity—than the mighty 88. First produced in 1933 as an anti-aircraft gun, it went through various modifications and was used against air, ground and sea targets—as a self-propelled gun, in the Tiger tank and in static emplacements. Whatever its role, it was superb. This is the Flak 41, mounted for anti-aircraft work. It could reach a height of 49,000 feet.

150-mm. K39 HOWITZER

This was the standard heavy support weapon in the artillery company of a German infantry regiment during the latter part of the war. As a field gun, it was towed into action. It was also used as a coastal defense gun. It could reach a top range of 27,000 yards with high-explosive or armor-piercing projectiles which weighed 94 to 99 pounds. When used as a field gun it was sprung on a split-trail, rubber-tired carriage.

THE JEEP

The ubiquitous jeep—otherwise described as the Truck, Utility, quarter-ton, 4x4 M38—served all services in most combat areas of World War II. It seemed to pop up everywhere, go almost anywhere, do almost anything but fight. It had its origin in a small runabout designed by the Bantam Car Company prior to 1939. When the U.S. Army sought a rugged field car, it tested and approved a prototype based on the Bantam. Contracts for mass production were given to the Willys Overland Company and later to Ford. Soon American, British and Canadian soldiers were singing the jeep's praises. It could make 55 miles an hour and, with four-wheel drive, was excellent at cross-country work. It could be fitted with wading equipment and eventually emerged in an amphibious version. A British general once expressed doubt that the jeep could have any valid military application. His name, mercifully, has been forgotten. The little vehicle was used for countless vital military tasks and became one of the war's best-known symbols.

VOLKSWAGEN LIGHT CAR

Adolf Hitler once decided that Germany should have a mass-produced "people's car." His whim never came to harvest in his lifetime but it did give the Germans their own wartime equivalent of the jeep. Based on a design by Dr. Ferdinand Porsche, several "people's car" prototypes were manufactured and a final version was selected before the war. A military model also emerged and a few proved themselves in the invasion of Poland in 1939. Eventually over 50,000 were built and used by the German Army. Like the jeep, the Volkswagen filled many roles: reconnaissance car (armed with the MG34 machine gun), staff car, stores carrier and light ambulance. The Type 82 shown here weighed 1400 pounds and could carry a load of over 1000 pounds. Its 24-horsepower engine gave a top speed of 50 miles an hour. It carried three or four men. Like the jeep, the Volkswagen car had an amphibious model. The waterborne version was driven by a three-blade propeller which engaged the end of the crankshaft by a sprocket-and-chain drive.

KANGAROO

The Kangaroo was born on the bloody road from Caen to Falaise during the Battle of Normandy in the summer of 1944. It was the brainchild of Lt. Gen. Guy Simonds, commander of the 2nd Canadian Corps. He was planning Operation Totalize, a major attack south of Caen, and he ordered that infantry accompanying tanks in the first assault "must go straight through with the armor in bullet- and splinter-proof vehicles." This, said Simonds, meant "unfrocking" some Priests, American-made self-propelled guns. Removing the 105-mm. guns and welding armor plate over the openings, a 250-man advanced work-shop, code-named Kangaroo, converted 76 Priests in three days. At 11:30 p.m. August 7, as Totalize began, the Kangaroo went into battle. Simonds' armored personnel carrier worked—then and later. Within a few months another version emerged, using the hull of the Ram, a Canadian tank that never got into action as a tank but did valuable service otherwise. Each Kangaroo carried 11 infantrymen plus its crew.

S.P.W.

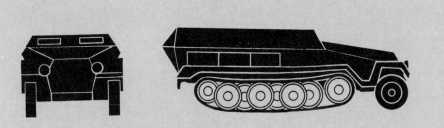

When Germany was working out her blitzkrieg tactics in the early '30s, she sought a lightly armored, semi-tracked vehicle that could carry infantry into battle—something better than the conventional truck. Several types were developed and one three-ton version became the S.P.W. *Schützenpanzerwagen* (infantry armored vehicle). With a loaded weight of eight tons, protected by 12-mm. armor plate, it carried 12 men at up to 30 miles an hour. It had two MG34 machine guns, one on a mount welded to the front of the chassis and one on an anti-aircraft pedestal in the rear of the vehicle. The carrier saw limited service in the 1939 invasion of Poland. Later it was used to carry panzer grenadiers, enabling them to keep up with the tanks, even off the roads. The 19-foot-long vehicle was also used as a command vehicle with built-in wireless, as an ambulance and as a self-propelled gun carriage. It gave effective service to the end of the war.

UNIVERSAL CARRIER

The Canadian Army's standard carrier was the Universal or Bren carrier, a lightly armored tracked vehicle which could carry four to six soldiers and their weapons. The men had all-round protection against small-arms fire but no overhead protection. The Universal could travel at 35 miles an hour and had many uses: reconnaissance, carrying ammunition or food or wounded men, transporting troops, mortars, machine guns or anti-tank guns and as a headquarters vehicle.

It evolved from the thinking of two Britons. Maj. G. (later Sir Giffard) Le Q. Martel built a small one-man tank in his garage in 1924. He and a retired army officer named Carden later convinced the War Office, and in time a machine-gun carrier came into production and from it was developed the Universal. More than 40,000 were built in the Commonwealth, many of them in Canada.

When used as a weapon carrier, the Universal was fitted with Vickers .303 machine guns or Bren light machine guns or 2-inch mortars. Some towed 6-pounder anti-tank guns.

One of the most useful versions was the Wasp flamethrower (shown here). An 80-gallon tank (A) of fras (jellied petroleum) was connected by hose to a projector (B) in which the fuel was retained under pressure. When the trigger (C) was pressed, nitrogen gas under pressure (D) forced fras from the projector. It was ignited by a gasoline jet below the projector and a spark which functioned before the fras jet was fully formed. The Wasp's three-man crew normally fired single short shots but could lengthen them or fire a stream of flame.

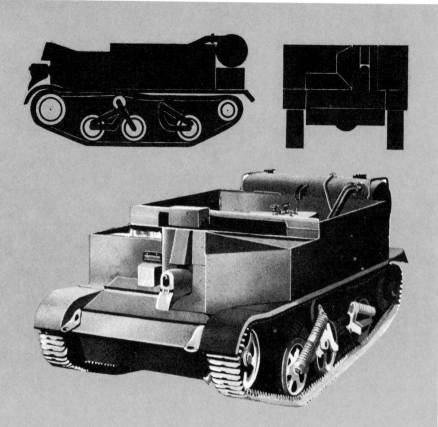

STAGHOUND ARMORED CAR

This product of General Motors was used by armored car and reconnaissance regiments for a variety of functions: raids, protection of road convoys and headquarters, patrols to get tactical intelligence. Armed with one 37-mm. gun and two .30 machine guns, the Staghound was manned by a crew of five and could hit a top speed of 55 m.p.h. Its maximum armor thickness was 1¼ inches.

PANZERSPAHWAGEN PUMA

An 11-ton, eight-wheeled armored car brought into German service in 1944, the Puma was designed to operate in very cold or very hot climates. It was primarily a reconnaissance vehicle but was also used for internal security duties. Top speed was 52 m.p.h. The Puma mounted a 50-mm. gun in a turret which could be swung in any direction. Its armor was 30 millimeters thick. Some models mounted a 75-mm. gun.

SHERMAN FIREFLY

Canadian armored formations in the United Kingdom trained in the British Churchill and Matilda tanks, the U.S. General Lee and the Canadian Ram. The Calgary Regiment, first unit of the Canadian Armored Corps to go into action, took the Churchill into battle for the first time, at Dieppe in August 1942. But it was the U.S. M4 medium tank—called the General Sherman—that Canadians used in Italy and northwest Europe. One troop of Canadian Shermans— of the 1st Hussars—got farther inland than any other Allied formation on June 6, 1944. The early 30-ton Sherman had a crew of five, a speed of 29 m.p.h. and a cruising range of 150 miles. It mounted a 75-mm. gun and two machine guns and was particularly reliable mechanically. But it was outclassed by the Germans' 56-ton Tiger with its heavy armor and 88-mm. gun. Later Shermans like the Firefly (right) mounted the British 17-pounder or the 105-mm. gun and became more of a match for the big Tiger (below).

TIGER TANK

Before the Canadians killed him on the road to Falaise in August 1944, a German officer named Michael Wittmann was credited with destruction of 138 tanks on the Russian and Normandy fronts. He got them as a crew commander in Tigers, the most powerful tanks the Allies faced. An experience of New Brunswick's 8th Hussars was typical. The first Tiger they encountered, in Italy in September 1944, knocked out four of their Shermans and there was nothing they could do about it. "We kept hitting it," said Maj. Cliff McEwen, "but our 75-mm. shells just bounced off." The 56-ton Tiger, wrote Alexander McKee in *Caen: Anvil of Victory,* was "like some impervious dinosaur out of prehistory." It had 100-mm. frontal armor and could make 12 m.p.h. across country, 23 on roads. It mounted the superb 88-mm. gun. But it had limitations due to its size, lack of mobility and slow-traversing turret. The lighter Allied tanks were often able to get in a quick first shot from front or rear. But once a Tiger started shooting, they were in trouble.

17-POUNDER (SELF-PROPELLED)

In a mobile war, guns that could move relatively fast on their own were valuable weapons. As German tanks grew in size and power, so did the Allies' anti-tank artillery and their emphasis on self-propelled guns. A British modification of a basic American design, this M10 self-propelled 17-pounder mounted its gun in a Sherman tank chassis with an open turret. It was used by anti-tank regiments, primarily in support of attacks by Sherman tanks armed with 75-mm. guns. In addition to the 17-pounder (76.2-mm.), it had a .50 machine gun for ground or anti-aircraft protection.

PANTHER TANK

Smaller but faster than the Tiger, the 50-ton Panther was nonetheless a giant among German armor—"one helluva tank," said one Canadian. To many, it was the best the Germans had. The low-slung Panther was conceived in Russia. Shaken by heavy armor losses against the Red Army's big T34, the Germans rushed design and construction of a tank that could best it. They got the Panther into action in 1943. With its long, high-velocity 75-mm. gun and two machine guns, its sloped armor and top speed of 30 m.p.h., it could outfight any Allied tank in a face-to-face encounter. But it had weaknesses. In Normandy a single Canadian Sherman, with a 17-pounder gun, took out six Panthers with seven shots, firing from the enemy's vulnerable flank. A Sherman could traverse its gun faster and fire three rounds to a Panther's one —and in any position, stopped or moving forward or backward. The Panther had trouble firing on the run.

THE PRIEST

The Americans called it the Gun Motor Carriage 105-mm. howitzer M7; the British nicknamed it the Priest because of its pulpit-like machine-gun mounting. It was a self-propelled gun first used by the British at El Alamein and later widely used elsewhere. Four Canadian artillery regiments, for instance, supported the Normandy D-Day landings by firing their Priests' howitzers from landing craft as they approached the beaches. Manned by a crew of seven, the 105-mm. howitzer fired a 33-pound high-explosive shell up to 11,500 yards. It could also be used against tanks. The Priest could make up to 24 m.p.h. The Canadians developed a counter-part called the Sexton, a self-propelled 25-pounder gun/howitzer.

STURMHAUBITZE 42

German self-propelled guns were mounted on half-tracks, on light or medium tank chassis and on armored vehicles captured in Poland, Czechoslovakia and France. An early model was the *Sturmgeschütz*, a short-barreled 75-mm. assault gun on a tank chassis. It was fully enclosed, highly mobile, low on the ground and hard to hit. To combat the Russian T34 tank a new *Sturmgeschütz* was developed, with a longer-ranged gun. Frontal armor was increased and a commander's cupola added. A variant was the *Sturmhaubitze 42*, a self-propelled 105-mm. assault howitzer —an equivalent of the Priest. It had a crew of four, top speed of 25 m.p.h. and a range of 13,400 yards. The Germans also had giant tank destroyers with the devastating 88-mm.

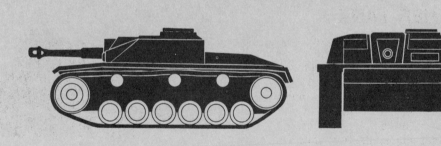

INSIDE THE SHERMAN

These cutaway illustrations show the positions of the crew of the Sherman medium tank (M4A2). The tank commander (A) is at the rear of the turret, just to the right of the 75-mm. gun guard. Almost directly in front of him is the gunner (B). The loader (C) sits to the left of the 75-mm. gun. In the left bow is the driver (D); the assistant driver (E) sits in the right bow, to the right of the transmission and behind the .30 bow machine gun. Access to the tank is by two hatches in the bow and a revolving hatch in the turret. For use in an emergency there is a quick-opening escape hatch (F) in the tank floor behind the assistant driver. The Sherman carried 97 rounds of 75-mm., 300 rounds of .50 for the anti-aircraft machine gun which in action was mounted on a revolving turret hatch ring, 6750

rounds of .30 for the two machine guns—one in the right bow, the other in the turret to the left of the 75-mm. There were also 12 hand grenades and 660 rounds of .45 for a Thompson submachine gun carried inside the turret.

Key: A—tank commander, B—gunner, C—loader, D—driver, E—assistant driver, F—emergency escape hatch in tank floor, G—.30 ammunition, G1—ready tray for .30 turret gun, G2—ready tray for .30 bow gun, H—.50 ammunition, I—ready rack on turret floor for eight 75-mm. shells, J—12 rounds of 75-mm. upright in ready clips around turret basket step, K—.45 ammunition in submachine-gun bracket above turret radio, L—steering brake levers, clutch, accelerator, M—gearshift (left) and parking brake, N—6-cylinder diesel engines.

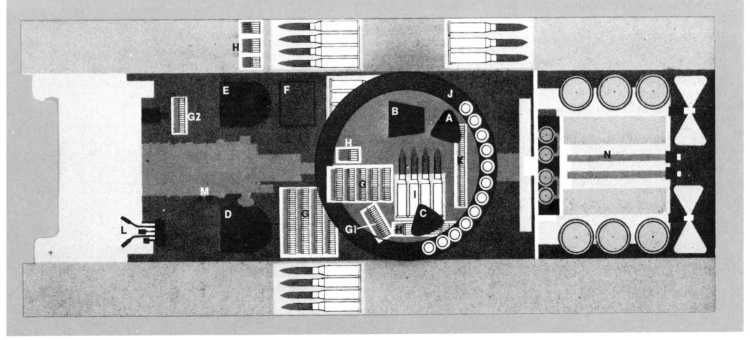

THE FUNNIES

Percy Hobart, one of prewar Britain's senior tank officers, became the father of the Funnies, a breed of special vehicles that were among the important by-products of the disastrous Dieppe raid of 1942. Ralph Allen wrote in *Ordeal by Fire:* "Dieppe got Corporal Hobart out of the Home Guard and back into the Regular Army and promoted him 11 grades to his old rank of major general. Working on his own and other people's ideas, he developed the swimming tank and the AVRE (Armored Vehicle Royal Engineers), a tank that could move up to a pillbox and either lob a lethal charge of explosive at it or clamp the explosive on the wall. He produced the Scorpion (or Flail), the Crocodile, the armored bulldozer and other tanks for bridging shell craters and ditches under fire." Four of the Funnies are on these pages.

ARMORED BULLDOZER

Among the unconventional and highly useful Funnies was the armored bulldozer, a conventional Caterpillar diesel tractor converted for military use. It was fitted with a 'dozer blade and was plated with armor to protect the engine and the driver. Assault engineers took their bulldozers ashore on D-Day in Normandy and cleared beach obstacles, worked with demolition teams to attack seawalls, constructed ramps to let tanks and vehicles get inland, cleared rubble and other obstacles, often under heavy fire. As the fighting moved on, the armored bulldozers proved invaluable for clearing streets in devastated towns, for filling bomb craters and removing road blocks. They carried no armament but they were vital engines of war. Chester Wilmot, in *The Struggle for Europe,* quotes Maj. Gen. Sir Percy Hobart's account of three top commanders' reaction to his Funnies: "Montgomery was most inquisitive. After thorough tests and searching questions he said in effect: 'I'll have this and this and this; but I don't want that or that.' Eisenhower was equally enthusiastic but not so discriminating. His response was, 'We'll take everything you can give us.' (U.S. Gen. Omar) Bradley appeared to be interested but, when asked what he wanted, replied, 'I'll have to consult my staff.' " Bradley and his staff eventually accepted the swimming tanks, says Wilmot, but not the rest of "Hobart's menagerie." British and Canadian formations used them all. The weird machines worked—and saved many lives.

CHURCHILL CROCODILE

The Crocodile flame tank was a conversion of the Churchill Mark VII, giving the Allies a new use for the old weapon of fire. This and other flamethrowers, spreading fear and despondency among their victims, were merely refinements of the boiling oil and flaming pitch of the Middle Ages. The use of tanks as flamethrowers was developed by the British Petroleum Warfare Department. The first experimental flame tanks accompanied the Canadians to Dieppe on August 19, 1942, but did not survive long enough to get into action. In 1943 the Churchill VII was selected as the standard flamethrower tank and named the Crocodile. Its flame gun, mounted in place of the hull machine gun, had a range of about 120 yards. The armored, 6½-ton trailer carried 400 gallons of flame fuel and six cylinders of compressed nitrogen which forced the fuel from trailer to gun. The Crocodile could fire continuously or 80 one-second bursts. A quick-release device enabled it to jettison its trailer and so revert to its normal tank role. Crocodiles were allocated to brigades or infantry battalions by squadrons or troops as circumstances demanded. A popular tactic for clearing built-up areas occupied by the enemy was for an infantry section to follow a Crocodile as it first fired a 75-mm. high-explosive round into a house, then a burst of flame through the hole it had made. Success on D-Day demanded that the Allies quickly break through German beach defenses. The Crocodile and other Funnies helped make that possible.

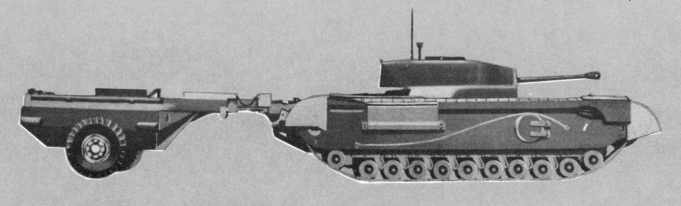

DUPLEX DRIVE (DD) TANK

The strange, powerful new vehicles that streamed to the beaches of Normandy on D-Day included what the Germans thought were small landing craft. They realized their mistake when the "landing craft" moved ashore and opened fire. These were the swimming tanks, amphibious Shermans that could make almost five knots in the water. They were called DD—for Duplex Drive, although the troops nicknamed them Donald Duck. The chassis of the Sherman was waterproofed and fitted with a collapsible canvas screen with rubber air tubes. The screen was secured to a deck around the tank hull and the tubes filled with compressed air. On inflation, the whole assembly was held in place by metal struts, giving the tank positive buoyancy with meager freeboard. The DD was moved by two propellers at the rear, connected to the tank's twin engines by bevel drives. It was steered by swiveling the screws. When the tank reached shore, the air tubes were deflated, the screen collapsed, the twin propellers retracted and it reverted to a normal tank. The 6th Canadian Armored Regiment (1st Hussars) launched two squadrons of DD tanks on D-Day and, despite a number foundering in the heavy seas, achieved marked success against German beach defenses.

SHERMAN CRAB

Another of the Funnies was the Crab, a minesweeping adaptation of the Sherman. Its power-operated flailing attachment could clear a 10-foot-wide path through a minefield at 1½ m.p.h. The flail was a rotor held between two girder assemblies extending from the front of the tank. Attached to the rotor were 43 chains, each with an iron ball at the other end. When the flail was rotated, by a special drive from the tank engine, the chains beat the ground and exploded mines to a depth of 10 inches. The Crab was equipped with station-keeping gear and minefield-marking equipment. Organized in troops of five, the Crabs had great success in Normandy and throughout the northwest European campaign. An improved version had a contouring device to adjust to ridges and furrows, giving extra protection to armor and infantry advancing through minefields.

During the mid-'30s, Britain discovered that Germany had secretly built an air force superior to the RAF. But Hermann Göring, the Luftwaffe chief, gave this assurance: "The drone of German fighters and defense squadrons will not disturb the symphony of peace. Germany means peace!"

The British air staff was unconvinced. It made two decisions that were to have a profound effect on the great air battles of the '40s.

The first was to replace the RAF's wooden biplane fighters with all-metal monoplanes armed with eight machine guns and capable of over 300 m.p.h.: the Hurricane and Spitfire that would save Britain from invasion.

The second was to issue specifications for a four-engine bomber with power-operated turret guns: this led ultimately to mass production of the Stirling, Halifax and Lancaster long-range bombers. This decision was based on belief that systematic bombing of plants and supply lines could destroy an enemy's capacity to wage war —and break civilian morale. Strategic bombing, it was thought, could win victory.

The Luftwaffe's first chief of staff, Gen. Walther Wever, also advocated a heavy bomber fleet. Two four-engine prototypes (Dornier 19 and Junkers 89) were built, but Wever's death in 1936 ended further development. The Germans decided they had neither time nor raw materials to build a strategic bomber fleet and that the Luftwaffe should concentrate on army and navy support. As a result, Germany built a *tactical* air force around the Junkers 87 dive-bomber, the Dornier 17 and Heinkel 111 medium bombers, the Junkers 52 troop transport and the versatile Junkers 88 which served as dive and level bomber, torpedo bomber, reconnaissance plane and night fighter. These aircraft, backed by the formidable Messerschmitt 109 fighter, formed the basis of an air force integrated with the army for the blitzkrieg to come.

When war came, the RAF and the Luftwaffe were both limited, for political reasons, to military targets, mainly warships and coastal installations. The RAF believed that a well-armed bomber group in tight formation could fly unescorted to daylight targets. On December 18, 1939, this belief was shattered. Half of the 24 Wellingtons sent to bomb warships off the German coast didn't get back. After this and other costly daylight raids, the RAF decided early in 1940 to attack at night.

On May 10, when Germany invaded Holland, Belgium and Luxembourg, Prime Minister Winston Churchill's cabinet hesitated to unleash British bombers for fear of inviting German retaliation and causing widespread civilian casualties. But four days later the Germans demanded that Rotterdam capitulate or be bombed. Parleys began between the Germans and the Dutch and the Germans finally sent a signal postponing the raid. But before the signal got through, half the German planes had dropped their bombs and the city was in flames. The next night RAF bombers attacked targets in Germany's Ruhr Valley.

The bombing war had begun, but not with the strategic offensive the peacetime RAF had planned. Bomber Command had a daily strength of only 300 to 400 frontline aircraft—far too few even if this force had not been reduced by navy and army demands. Its aircraft were mainly two-engine Blenheims, Hampdens, Whitleys and Wellingtons, with light bombloads. More serious still was the difficulty most aircrews

> Their prestige stood high, for they were the defenders of the people and sometimes they, and they alone, stood between victory and defeat. They lived a strange life, which alternated between short periods of intense excitement in the air, when they did not have enough time, and long spells on the ground, when they had too much. Once in the air they had the gift of becoming part of their fighters. Their morale was very high. In adversity they were bigger than their normal selves. Their devotion was well hidden beneath an outward flippancy.
>
> **Air Vice-Marshal J. E. Johnson in *Full Circle, The Story of Air Fighting***

had in finding and hitting targets by night. A 1941 survey revealed that, of those claiming to have hit the target, only one crew in three had in fact bombed within five miles of it—and over the heavily defended Ruhr, only one in ten had done so. Until crews got accurate navigation and aiming aids, it was futile to attack an individual factory or oil plant except on clear moonlit nights.

In February 1942 Bomber Command switched from precision bombing to area bombing. The targets were whole towns and industrial centers, so that even bombs which missed military targets might still dislocate public services, destroy housing, weaken morale and slow war production.

The Search for Accuracy

To improve bombing accuracy the bomber crew was reorganized: the second pilot was replaced by a flight engineer; a bomb-aimer was added; the observer, renamed navigator, gave up his other duties of bomb-aiming and gunnery to concentrate on navigation. In August 1942 Bomber Command created a pathfinder force to mark the bombers' route and target with flares. A year later it introduced master bombers to control target marking and direct incoming bombers throughout the raid.

In March 1942 a new radio navigation aid called Gee came into service. It enabled the navigator to fix his position from radio impulses transmitted from ground stations in England. The Germans countered with Heinrich, a transmitter which jammed Gee signals once the aircraft crossed the occupied coast. But Gee remained useful, giving a final fix before a bomber entered enemy territory and a homing signal on its return.

More important, perhaps, Gee enabled the Command to use a bomber-stream technique to overwhelm Germany's early-warning radar system. The German network stretched along the occupied coast and the approaches to the Ruhr in an interlocking chain of radar stations about 20 miles apart. Each had a 75-mile Freya radar and two short-range Giant Würzburg radars. As a bomber approached, the Freya reported its position to a controller who alerted the anti-aircraft defenses and dispatched a radar-equipped night fighter to orbit the station. Now the two Würzburgs took over —one tracked the bomber's approach, the other guided the night fighter until its own two-mile Lichtenstein radar could pick up the bomber. The system had a serious drawback: each station could engage only one bomber at a time. Nevertheless it worked because the Allied bombers flew independently—navigation was too imprecise for concentrated formations.

This situation changed dramatically with Gee navigation. On May 30, 1942, the night of the first 1000-plane raid, the bomber-stream tactic was used for the first time. The bombers all took the same route to Cologne, flying in waves at timed intervals and at staggered heights. Instead of lasting 7 hours, the raid was completed in 2½. Although 4 aircraft were lost in collisions over the target and 39 were destroyed, mostly by night fighters, 910 of the 1096 bombers that took off actually bombed the target. They caused almost as much damage as all previous raids on Germany. Said Churchill: "This is the herald of what Germany will receive, city by city, from now on."

But Bomber Command had scraped together planes for the Cologne raid by borrowing from Coastal Command and training units. Not until early 1943 could it mount a sustained offensive. Even then its frontline strength of 550 aircraft was only half of what its chief, Air Chief Marshal Sir Arthur Harris, considered essential. But about 65 percent of this force was made up of the long-awaited four-engine Stirling, Halifax and Lancaster bombers, and their numbers kept increasing. Within a year almost the entire daily strength of some 950 aircraft were heavy bombers, mostly the celebrated Lancasters.

The heavies could carry bombloads up to 14,000 pounds and the monthly tonnage increased greatly. The bombs themselves were bigger and more powerful and included Block Busters ranging from 2000 to 12,000 pounds, thin-cased bombs with a great blasting effect.

Almost every aircraft also carried the improved Mark XIV bombsight which automatically computed much of the required data and allowed the aircraft to take gentle evasive action against anti-aircraft fire right up to bomb release. Developments in aerial cameras and photo interpretation permitted scientific analysis of bombing results.

In the spring of 1943, two revolutionary radar aids came into service. Oboe enabled transmitters in England to direct a bomber to its target and radio a bomb-release signal. It was highly accurate and had a range of 270 miles, easily covering the Ruhr. Since each pair of stations could control only six aircraft an hour, Oboe was limited to the target-marking pathfinder

force with its fast, high-altitude Mosquito fighter-bomber—one of the most versatile aircraft of the war.

H2S, the second radar aid, was carried aboard the aircraft. Mounted downward, it enabled the navigator to "see" through dark and cloud by bouncing radio signals off the ground. The reflected signals reproduced a map-like pattern of the ground on a cathode ray tube, similar to a TV screen. The navigator could scan the territory below, fix his position and identify the target.

German Stuka dive-bombers on their way to attack British tanks in North Africa in November 1941. "Troops subjected to the Stuka," says the official *RAF Middle East,* "frankly detested it. Nevertheless, against targets of reasonable dispersal in the desert, the Stuka was a failure. . . . the Stuka in flight is almost defenseless, needing the strongest fighter cover, which even so never debarred the desert fighters from the satisfaction of a Stuka party."

The Strategic Offensive

In March 1943 the strategic offensive against Germany got underway. From a technical standpoint it became a battle of wits to master the airwaves. One RAF method was to jam the radar of German night fighters and anti-aircraft guns. Mandrel, a British airborne noisemaker, obliterated Freya signals. Tinsel, hooked up to the bomber's engines, broadcast loud engine noises over the enemy ground-to-air radio communications. To make jamming difficult, the Germans widened the range of the radio frequencies they used.

Then came a breakthrough. After long debate, the RAF was permitted to use Window. Short metal foil strips were dropped in clusters to produce hundreds of "blips" on German radar screens. One controller said it seemed that "the air was filled with bombers." Window was no surprise to German scientists. They invented a similar device but were forbidden to experiment—to keep the RAF from learning the secret.

Window was first used in the great firestorm raids on Hamburg in July 1943. It paralyzed German defenses by disrupting radar control of guns, searchlights and fighters. But as usual, the Germans quickly recovered.

First they hunted blindly. Day fighters were sent up at night to circle high above target areas and dive on bombers silhouetted in the glare of searchlights, flares and fires. Night fighters (Me 110s, Ju 88s and the new Heinkel 219s) were told to forget their radar and were directed to concentrations of Window, pathfinder markers and bomber approach routes to seek out the raiders visually. On the clear summer nights of 1943, this tactic was often successful.

The Luftwaffe also hit back by letting the Allied bombers betray themselves: listening posts with a radar called Korfu tracked the bombers' H2S transmissions. The fighters were placed under one controller who broadcast orders over high-powered, multi-channeled radio stations and directed them to the bomber streams. Then Naxos-Z, the airborne counterpart of Korfu, enabled the fighters to home on the bombers.

The RAF countered with a new bomber group, No. 100, to jam these broadcasts with special transmitters. Corona was operated from ground stations in England; Airborne Cigar and Special Tinsel were carried in aircraft flying with the bombers.

Over these transmitters 100 Group broadcast a barrage of noise. They also issued bogus instructions in German. One night the German controller started swearing and shouting, "Don't be led astray by the enemy." The Corona voice replied: "The Englishman is now swearing." To which the German retorted: "It's not the Englishman, it's me!" When the Germans brought in a woman to broadcast orders, 100 Group had a German-speaking woman mimic her voice and issue false orders. The Germans tried issuing instructions in Morse code; the RAF replied with meaningless Morse signals on German frequencies. The Germans switched to coded musical messages over Stuttgart radio. The RAF jammed them with a powerful transmitter called Dartboard.

Nevertheless, the German fighters with their new Naxos homing device were getting into bomber streams and scoring kill after kill. The bombers fought back by installing Monica, a device which set off a series of blips when an aircraft approached. Unfortunately the alarm went off at the approach of Allied planes too. Boozer proved better; it gave a red light warning whenever a fighter got on a bomber's tail.

No. 100 Group also started to hunt the hunters. Long-range Mosquitos were equipped with Serrate, a radar that homed on Naxos transmissions. One tactic was to patrol German airfields and attack when night fighters took off or came in to land. But again the Germans invented a countermeasure: SN-2, a night-fighter radar that operated on a frequency which could not be jammed by Window and was impervious to Serrate.

In late March 1944, Bomber Command broke off the offensive to give tactical support for the forthcoming invasion of France. In the previous four months, Germany had destroyed more than 1000 Allied bombers and damaged 1600—a deadly casualty rate.

Bomber Command now struck at German defenses along the Atlantic Wall and at the rail and road network linking Germany to the invasion coast. After D-Day the Command gave direct support to the armies as a sort of flying artillery, attacking day and night and usually in smaller formations than before. Bomber casualties were relatively light.

In September, Germany became the target again but the situation was very different now. German defenses were crumbling. The loss of large parts of western Europe had opened a big gap in their radar

system. There was a shortage of trained Luftwaffe pilots and little fuel for training more. The Allied air forces ruled the air and grew ever stronger.

In October 1944 Bomber Command had a daily frontline strength of 470 Halifaxes and 870 Lancasters—some of the latter equipped to carry the 12,000-pound Tallboy and 22,000-pound Grand Slam bombs. In addition it had 120 Mosquitos for target marking and night-fighter operations.

And bombing was more accurate. One reason was the development of daylight precision attacks based on a new blind-bombing radar aid called G-H. Another was the visual marking technique developed by 5 Group for night raids.

A typical attack opened with high-flying, Oboe-equipped Mosquitos illuminating the target area. The master bomber dived on the target and at very low level dropped a red fire marker to indicate the aiming point. Other aircraft, meanwhile, flew over the target at bombing height to calculate the wind's speed and direction. This information was radioed to the approaching bomber stream so that bomb-aimers could adjust their sights. If the aiming-point fire became obscured during the attack, the pathfinder force flew in again to lay an offset marker. The relationship of this marker to the original aiming point was worked out and a new "false wind" was calculated and broadcast to the bombers. Now bombs aimed at the offset marker fell on target.

No. 100 Group developed a sophisticated system of jamming and deception. On a major raid a force of Mandrel-equipped aircraft flew ahead to jam the German early-warning radar. Other aircraft, carrying a powerful transmitter called Jostle, obliterated ground-to-air radio communications. Behind this jamming screen—sometimes up to 80 miles wide—the main bomber stream moved in. Soon small formations split off from the stream and, cascading clouds of Window, made feint attacks to deceive the German fighter controller. Mosquito fighters, equipped with a homing device that countered SN-2, ranged far ahead seeking night fighters. By VE-Day, 236 German fighters had been destroyed by this system.

These measures were so successful that by 1945 Bomber Command could hit any target in Germany hard and accurately with losses as low as one percent or less.

In the last seven months of war, Bomber Command dropped almost 400,000 tons of bombs. This massive assault, coupled with that of the U.S. Army Air Force, knocked out Germany's oil supplies, immobilized her transportation system and left many cities in ruins. By mid-April there was no important target left. The strategic air offensive was over.

Canadian airmen had been in bombing action from the beginning—some 200 of them helped bomb enemy invasion ports during the 1940 Battle of Britain. The first RCAF bomber squadrons were formed in June 1941, among them 405 Squadron, which later became a leading unit in the famous pathfinder force. An estimated 500 Canadians flew on the first 1000-bomber raid, on Cologne. On January 1, 1943, eight Canadian squadrons were banded together as No. 6 (RCAF) Group of RAF Bomber Command. This group fought in every phase of the RAF's offensive of 1943-44. Three squadrons also took part in the invasion of Sicily and Italy. By war's end No. 6 had grown to 14 squadrons.

The Fighters' War

In July 1940 the Luftwaffe received alarming reports from its radio monitoring service. The air was alive with signals radiating from Britain. British voices on a high-frequency radio were directing formations of RAF fighters toward unseen waves of attacking German bombers. The Germans realized they were up against something they hadn't dreamed the RAF possessed: a system of early-warning radar and fighter control. This interception system saved Britain from invasion, won the first strategic air battle in history and changed the course of the war.

The key was radar, then called RDF (radio direction finding). Experiments in tracking aircraft by radio signals transmitted from a ground station had begun in 1935. By 1940, Britain had set up a coastal chain of radar stations: high-level radar to detect raiders up to 100 miles away; low-level to track low-flying aircraft within 50 miles. The network broadcast radio signal beams. Aircraft flying into them reflected the signals back to the radar stations where they were recorded as blips of light on cathode ray tubes.

These blips recorded the distance, height, bearing and numbers of the raiders. To identify friend from foe, RAF aircraft carried small transmitters whose signals produced different blips. The enemy's position was reported to Fighter Command and from there to fighter groups and sector stations and to Anti-Aircraft Command and Royal Observer Corps centers.

Fifty thousand civilian observers were the inner eyes of the defense system. Scattered throughout the countryside, they worked in pairs in small huts, using binoculars and a simple sighting device mounted on a grid map. When aircraft were sighted, the observers phoned their height and position to a local center. There a team of plotters collated reports, worked out the raiders' bearing and numbers and informed Fighter Command.

A Lancaster bomber over Cap Gris Nez during a raid on the French coast September 26, 1944.

At Fighter Command, a picture built up as plotters moved markers representing hostile and friendly aircraft across a map. In a gallery above, a fighter controller studied the situation. Similar maps were watched at fighter group and sector control rooms. On the airfields, alerted squadrons stood by their aircraft.

When a squadron took off, its sector station controller gave instructions over high-frequency radio telephone. R/T enabled controller and pilot to communicate and its transmission allowed direction-finding operators to keep a fix on the aircraft's position. A device automatically switched on the plane's transmitter for 14 seconds every minute. The planes were controlled in fours, each automatically transmitting in rotation, while a control room clock recorded the data: R/T enabled the controller

to steer the squadron toward the enemy relieving the pilots from navigation an position fixing. Knowing both the raider bearing and position and the fighter's position, the control room could work out steering angle to bring the planes on a interception course.

On August 10, 1940, the eve of the mai Battle of Britain assault, the RAF had 70 Hurricanes and Spitfires and some 40 two seater Blenheims and Defiants to oppos 805 Messerschmitt 109E fighters, 224 two engine Me 110 fighters and 1259 bomber A third of the RAF force, however, ha to be held back to guard the Midlands an the north. The RAF's main fighters wei the Hurricane I and II and the Spitfire and II, both armed with eight Brownin .303 machine guns. The Me 109 had tw 7.9-mm. machine guns and two 20-mm annon. These cannon could do more damage than the .303s but the Brownings had faster rate of fire, giving them a better hance of scoring with a short burst. The Hurricane made up two thirds of the RAF orce and was a tough, reliable fighter with xcellent maneuverability at 20,000 feet nd a sturdy gun platform. It was slower han the Me 109 but could outturn it. So ould the Spitfire, and it was as fast as the erman fighter. Although the Me 109 could

utclimb and outdive both RAF aircraft, s lack of range was a disadvantage. Whenver possible, the Hurricanes were dispatchd to intercept bombers while the abler pitfires flew top cover to tackle high-flying le 109 escorts.

The unwieldy two-engine Me 110 fighter scort proved no match for the RAF fight-s. The bombers—Heinkel 111, Junkers 8 and Dornier 17 and 215—were also easy ame for RAF planes. The Germans' big-est disappointment was the Junkers 87 ive-bomber, the vaunted Stuka. Although accessful in Poland and France, it was so adly mauled over Britain that it was with-rawn.

German pilots had tested and proved heir tactics in the Spanish civil war. They sed loose, easy-to-maintain formations, ying in stepped-up heights to provide bet-ter lookout and give one another cover. The basic element was two planes: one led and navigated, the other guarded its tail. Two pairs, about 200 yards apart, formed a *Schwarm* (section).

The rigid formations the RAF used at the start of the war were eventually discarded in favor of less vulnerable, more effective formations such as the Germans had perfected.

Fighter Command, outnumbered as it was, achieved victory for several reasons. Radar and fighter control prevented the Luftwaffe from gaining surprise and let the RAF conserve its strength. Fighter Command was able to send up squadrons when they could hit hardest and wisely refused to be drawn into a battle of attrition. Fighting over home ground, the RAF could keep its planes in the air longer and save many of its downed pilots.

The Luftwaffe committed major blunders. It tried to fight a strategic battle with a tactical force. Lacking four-engine bombers, it attacked with under-armed two-engine planes too limited in range and bombload. Its unwieldy Me 110 fighter was useless as a bomber escort; Me 109 escorts lacked range and were often tied to the bombers instead of being free to make use of height and speed. But its chief blunder was made September 7 when it called off attacks on RAF airfields and turned on London. At that stage Fighter Command was in serious trouble. From August 24 to September 6 it had lost 295 aircraft destroyed and 171 damaged. Worse, it was losing pilots at the rate of 120 a week—out of a strength of just under 1000. With the end of the airfield attacks, Fighter Command regained the initiative.

The Night Fighters

Heavy losses in day raids on Britain forced Germany into night bombing. In these attacks the Germans used radar aids and bombing tactics that Britain did not develop for almost two years. Their devastating effect was demonstrated at Coventry the night of November 14, 1940.

The raid was led by a pathfinder squadron flying Heinkel 111s equipped with incendiary marker bombs and a radar called X-Gerat. It used radio signal beams to guide the pathfinders to the target and signal the navigator to release his bombs. Fires started by incendiaries guided the rest of the 437 bombers to the target.

Britain fought night raiders by jamming German radar signals and by using radar-equipped night-fighter squadrons. When an enemy aircraft was tracked by ground radar, a patrolling night fighter was directed toward it until its own radar homed on the enemy plane. This was theory—in practice night fighting was a frustrating, dangerous job. Radar signals were difficult to interpret. Flying and landing in winter weather was hazardous. Navigation and airfield approach aids were scarce and runways were poorly lit. More crews were lost to accidents than enemy action.

Blenheims, Defiants and Havocs were pressed into the night-fighter force. But results were poor until the two-seater Bristol Beaufighter arrived with its Mark IV airborne radar. It could pick up an aircraft at four miles and track it to eyesight range. The Beaufighter, backed by anti-aircraft artillery, began to take its toll of the raiders. The battle, however, ended inconclusively.

In May 1941 the Luftwaffe withdrew its bomber groups for Hitler's June 22 attack on Russia. The blitz on Britain ended. It had killed 40,000 people and damaged more than a million homes. The Germans had lost some 600 aircraft in night attacks. Some bombing continued but it never again reached the same intensity. Britain brought in more night-fighter units (including Canada's Lynx, Nighthawk and Cougar squadrons), improved its radar defenses and replaced the Beaufighter with the Mosquito. But the real solution lay in carrying the war to the enemy.

The Time of Attack

In 1941, with a growing number of Canadian squadrons in its ranks, Fighter Command went on the offensive, using two basic approaches. Rhubarbs were low-level strafing attacks by two or four aircraft; Circuses were large fighter sweeps involving up to 300 fighters plus light and medium bombers. Their aim was to hit targets, lure the Luftwaffe into battle and force the Germans to maintain air defenses in the west, thus relieving pressure on other fronts. Although the RAF lost more fighters than the Germans in the first two years, the attacks were continued with increasing intensity until the invasion.

During this period the Germans introduced a new fighter—the Focke-Wulf 190. It outclassed the current Spitfire for almost two years. Some 30 to 50 m.p.h. faster than the Spitfire V, the FW 190 was almost effortless to handle, even at high altitude, and could make turns that would have torn the wings off another fighter. The FW 190 had a top speed of 408 m.p.h.; the long-nosed FW 190D could do 426.

Britain's designers countered with the Spitfire IX, which had a speed of 408 m.p.h. To combat low-flying FW 190 sneak raiders, the British introduced the Spitfire XII, a low-altitude interceptor and ground-attack plane.

Meanwhile, the RAF was providing tactical support for the army and navy on other fronts. In North Africa the fighter squadrons of the Desert Air Force—including Canada's 417 Squadron—moved where the army moved. During the desert battles of 1942-43, the RAF's main fighters were Spitfire V interceptors, long-range Bristol Beaufighters, Curtiss Kittyhawks, Hurricane IIA fighter-bombers, and the tank-busting Hurricane IIDs equipped with two heavy 40-mm. cannon carried under strengthened wings. Flying at almost ground level, the Hurricane IIDs were so successful in anti-tank warfare that they were nick-named the "flying can-openers."

Fighter planes in the desert had many roles: air-to-air fighting, dive-bombing, ground strafing, reconnaissance patrols, bomber escort. Even the thoroughbred Spitfire had to conform. Racks were fitted under the fuselage and wings to carry bombs. To boost its ground-attack performance, the tips of the famous elliptical wings were clipped straight to improve rolling characteristics at low heights and the engine's supercharger was cropped so that the plane developed its best speed at about 8000 feet.

Close-support tactics were perfected in 1943, when the Desert Air Force and Eighth Army were fighting in Italy. An RAF controller and army liaison officer set up a mobile observation post which kept radio contact with fighter patrols. When the army asked for support, the controller radioed the fighter-bombers—the Cab Rank —giving them the target. Within minutes they attacked.

This system was used with great success by the RAF's 2nd Tactical Air Force at the time of the Normandy invasion. The force had five tasks: to attack coastal defenses and transportation targets before the invasion, give air cover to the invading troops, harass enemy reinforcements, gain air superiority and support the ground forces by bombing and strafing. Control of the air passed to the Allies on D-Day and was never lost. The Luftwaffe was outnumbered and outclassed. There were many skirmishes but few large aerial battles.

Fifteen Canadian fighter squadrons fought in northwest Europe. Three served with 39 Reconnaissance Wing, flying camera-equipped Spitfires and Mustangs. Eventually the wing was able to supply frontline army officers with photographs of enemy positions taken only a few hours before they were to be attacked.

Four other Canadian squadrons served in 143 Wing. They flew the Hawker Typhoon, one of the hardest-hitting of all Allied ground-attack planes. Originally designed as a fighter interceptor, it was rushed into service before being fully tested. The Typhoon proved a poor performer at high altitude and also suffered engine and airframe failures, but its thick wings made it an excellent low-level fighter-bomber. In this role the Typhoon carried a 2000-pound bombload, more than any other single-seater fighter. As an alternative, the Typhoon could be armed with eight 3-inch rockets. Combined with the plane's four 20-mm. cannon, they provided a devastating punch.

Eight Canadian squadrons formed the RCAF's 126 and 127 wings. Their planes were Mark IX, XIV and XVI Spitfire interceptors armed with two 20-mm. cannon and four .303 machine guns. They also operated as fighter-bombers, carrying 1000-pound bombloads. The two wings destroyed 545 aircraft—including the first Me 262 jet fighter shot down.

Jets and Rockets

The superb Me 262 first appeared over Holland in October 1944. No Allied fighter could touch its speed of 540 m.p.h. or its performance. It was fortunate that, like Germany's Me163 Komet, the first rocket-powered fighter, it appeared too late in the war to make a difference.

Britain also developed a jet fighter, the Gloster Meteor. The Mark III had a top speed of 493 m.p.h. at 30,000 feet, but it did not come into service until mid-April 1945. The Mark I Meteor, however, did see action against the German V-1 rocket missiles, the buzz bombs.

The jet-propelled V-1s, each carrying a ton of explosives, were first fired in June 1944 from launching sites in the Pas de Calais. They flew straight for London at 400 m.p.h. The British set up a ring of radar-controlled anti-aircraft guns and barrage balloons around southeast England. On the outer line of defense were the fighters—Spitfires, Tempests, Mosquitos, Meteors—whose job was to intercept and ex-plode the flying bombs over the Channel. Tactics evolved in action. A chase from astern proved futile unless the fighter could increase its speed by diving. The best method was to fly ahead of the bomb on a parallel course and wait for it to overtake before firing. Some pilots, when out of ammunition, placed a wingtip under the bomb's wing and tumbled it off course or flew ahead on the same course so that the aircraft's slipstream unbalanced the missile and sent it out of control. Of some 8000 bombs launched, only 2400 got through the defenses—but they killed 6184 persons. Three RCAF squadrons (402, 409, 418) knocked out 97 bombs—82 were destroyed by the Mosquitos of 418 Squadron. The menace ended in September when the First Canadian Army overran the launching sites.

Then came the V-2 ballistic missiles—silent, deadly, unseen as they hurtled through the skies at 3500 m.p.h. Launched from mobile pads in Holland, the rockets were aimed at England and Belgium. Conventional aircraft could do nothing except try to destroy their bases. A thousand V-2s fell on England, killing 2800. They killed 8000 Belgians before they were silenced by the liberation of Holland.

The air war was fought mainly with weapons in existence or under study in 1939 and modified to meet the tactical needs of the moment. The jet fighter and rocket missile, however, opened a new era. Overnight the piston-engined aircraft was outmoded. The V-2 pointed the way to the guided intercontinental rocket and the space-age missile. At war's end the Allies found some surprising aerodynamic jet developments on German drawing boards—vertical takeoff aircraft, swivel-wing fighters, four-engine delta wing bombers and a project for a two-stage, 3000-mile rocket to bombard the U.S.A. from Germany.

But the most devastating weapon of all was unveiled by the Americans on August 6, 1945: the atomic bomb dropped on Hiroshima. It ended one world war and opened man's eyes to what another would bring. Faced with the prospect of nuclear annihilation, the world at last was confronted with the ultimate question: how could mankind effectively disarm the most deadly weapon of all—man himself?

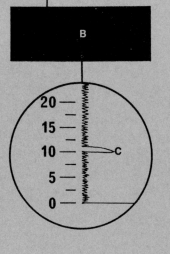

RADAR: THE INVISIBLE EYE

Radar (for radio detection and ranging) is a method of locating an object by "bombarding" it with radio waves and measuring the time taken for the waves to go out and bounce back to the sender. Since radio waves travel at a constant speed of 186,000 miles a second, a target's position can be fixed with great accuracy. One of the most vital tools of the war, radar was employed by both sides. The Allies used it to hunt U-boats, detect enemy aircraft, control gun fire, guide bomber planes to their targets, and for many other tasks. Radar helped win the Battle of Britain, where its use as a military tool was fully tested for the first time in action. During this battle a chain of coastal radar stations provided early warning of enemy planes coming across the English Channel and North Sea and gave the RAF time to send up fighters to intercept. The radar's antenna (A) sent out radio waves in very short pulses. When an aircraft flew into the beam it reflected some of the waves back to the antenna. The transmitter/receiver (B) amplified the reflected signal and passed it to a cathode ray tube (like a TV picture tube). There it appeared as a blip of light on a screen marked off in miles: the blip (C) shows the target is ten miles away. Radar also estimated the number of targets and gave their bearing and height.

DE HAVILLAND TIGER MOTH

Thousands of Canadians made their first solo flights in the little two-seater Tiger Moth, the chief elementary training plane of the British Commonwealth Air Training Plan flying schools. Test-flown in 1931, it was already famous as a trainer and stunt plane when war began. Canada built some 2000 Moths. Canadian design changes included a sliding canopy to keep out bitter prairie winter winds and a shortened raked-forward undercarriage to prevent the plane nosing over when brakes were applied too sharply— as they often were! About two thirds of the men who washed out (failed) the pilot's course did so at the elementary stage.

Canadian-built de Havilland Tiger Moth 82C. Two-seat elementary trainer. Wood-and-metal construction, fabric covered. Maximum speed 109 m.p.h. at 1000 ft.

NORTH AMERICAN HARVARD

The wartime RCAF did not use an intermediate trainer. If a student fighter pilot survived 60 hours on the Tiger Moth, he graduated to the Harvard advanced trainer, better known as the Yellow Peril. It was quite a jump—from a 145-horsepower to a 600-horsepower plane that was fully aerobatic and to a cockpit full of strange instruments that the student had to be able to locate blindfolded. Fighter pilot students learned the hard way. Instructors were told to "let the pupil get into a mess and find the remedy himself." It took some 22 weeks and cost about $21,000 to train a pilot.

North American Harvard IIA. Two-seat advanced trainer. All-metal stressed-skin construction. Maximum speed 205 m.p.h. at 5000 ft.

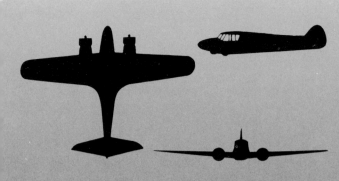

AVRO ANSON

After elementary flying, pupils judged to be "bomber pilot material" graduated to training in two-engine planes like the Anson. It was also used to school navigators, bomb-aimers and gunners. In 1940 Canada's air training plan suffered a severe setback when Britain, hard pressed to defend herself, was unable to supply Ansons to the RCAF. Canada met the emergency by setting up plants to build Ansons redesigned to take the U.S.-built Jacobs engine. Although fighter pilot pupils derided the Anson as "10,000 aircraft parts flying in close formation," it was most reliable. Bomber crew pupils called it "Faithful Annie."

Avro Anson reconnaissance plane and trainer. Fabric-covered metal fuselage but construction varied. Canadian Ansons had Jacobs or Wright engines. Maximum speed (Mark I) 188 m.p.h. at 7000 ft.

FAIREY BATTLE

The Battle saw action as a light bomber in May 1940 and two RAF men won the war's first air V.C.s in one while attempting to blow up vital bridges and stem the German advance into Belgium. But already the Battle was obsolete and it spent the rest of its days as a trainer. Many were sent to Canada for use in air gunnery schools. Students fired from the rear cockpit at target kites towed by another plane. The fine or "rumble" for drilling bullet holes in one's own tail plane was a dollar a hole. It took some 24 weeks to train a Wag (wireless operator air gunner) at a cost of about $8750.

Fairey Battle light bomber (equipped here as an air gunnery trainer). All-metal stressed-skin construction. Maximum speed 241 m.p.h. at 13,000 ft.

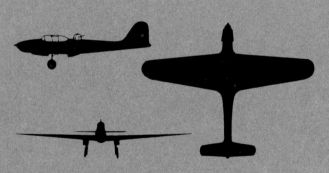

HAWKER HURRICANE

Designed in 1934 by Sydney Camm, the Hurricane was the RAF's first monoplane fighter. Some 12,700 were built—1400 in Canada. Mark Brown, the first Canadian World War II ace, flew a Hurricane over France in 1940, and the RCAF's No. 1 Squadron flew them during the Battle of Britain—when Hurricane pilots destroyed more aircraft than all other defenses combined. Outdated as an interceptor by 1942, the Hurricane fought on as a fighter-bomber and ground attack plane, serving on every front, including Russia. It was even launched by catapult from merchant ship aircraft carriers defending Atlantic convoys.

Hawker Hurricane single-seat fighter. Metal airframe, metal-covered wings, fabric-covered fuselage. Maximum speed (Mark I) 316 m.p.h. at 17,500 ft. Eight .303 guns.

MESSERSCHMITT 109

The Luftwaffe's chief single-seat fighter was the Me 109. Designed by Prof. Willy Messerschmitt in 1934, it was battle tested in the Spanish civil war by German volunteers flying in the Condor Legion, among them Adolf Galland and Werner Mölders, who became famous World War II aces. The main variant flown in the Battle of Britain was the Me 109E. Called the Emil, it was a great fighter plane—faster than the Hurricane, as fast as the Spitfires I and II, and able to outclimb and outdive both. The Me 109 served throughout the war. Some 33,000 were built—more than any other fighter.

Messerschmitt 109E single-seat fighter. All-metal stressed-skin construction. Maximum speed 354 m.p.h. at 12,300 ft. Two 7.9-mm. guns and two 20-mm. cannon.

VICKERS SUPERMARINE SPITFIRE

At the height of the Battle of Britain, Nazi air chief Hermann Göring angrily asked Adolf Galland what he needed for victory. Piqued, the German ace retorted: "The Spitfire!" It was a well deserved tribute. Designed by Reginald Mitchell, the Spitfire was a descendant of the S-6B, the 400-m.p.h. prewar racing plane that won the Schneider Trophy. The basic design was so good that the Spitfire remained Britain's top fighter throughout the war. Produced in 22 marks, it underwent some 40 major changes which raised its power 100%, its rate of climb 80% and its top speed from 355 to 454 m.p.h.

Supermarine Spitfire single-seat fighter and fighter-bomber. All-metal stressed-skin construction. Maximum speed 355 to 454 m.p.h. depending on mark. Armament varied: shown here, two .5 guns, two 20-mm. cannon.

FOCKE-WULF 190

In 1941 Allied pilots on fighter sweeps over France were badly mauled by a new German fighter—Kurt Tank's Focke-Wulf 190. Sleeker and faster than the Me 109, it quickly proved it could outperform the Commonwealth's best, the Spitfire V. For two years it reigned supreme and during the Dieppe raid of August 1942 a mixed force of FW 190s and Me 109s shot down Allied planes at a rate of two to one. But the Spitfire was not to be beaten. With the introduction in 1943 of the Spitfire IX and the Spitfire XIV, the Focke-Wulf 190 was finally matched.

Focke-Wulf 190D-9 single-seat fighter and fighter-bomber. All-metal stressed-skin construction. Maximum speed 397 m.p.h. at 32,000 ft. Two 13-mm. guns, two 20-mm. cannon.

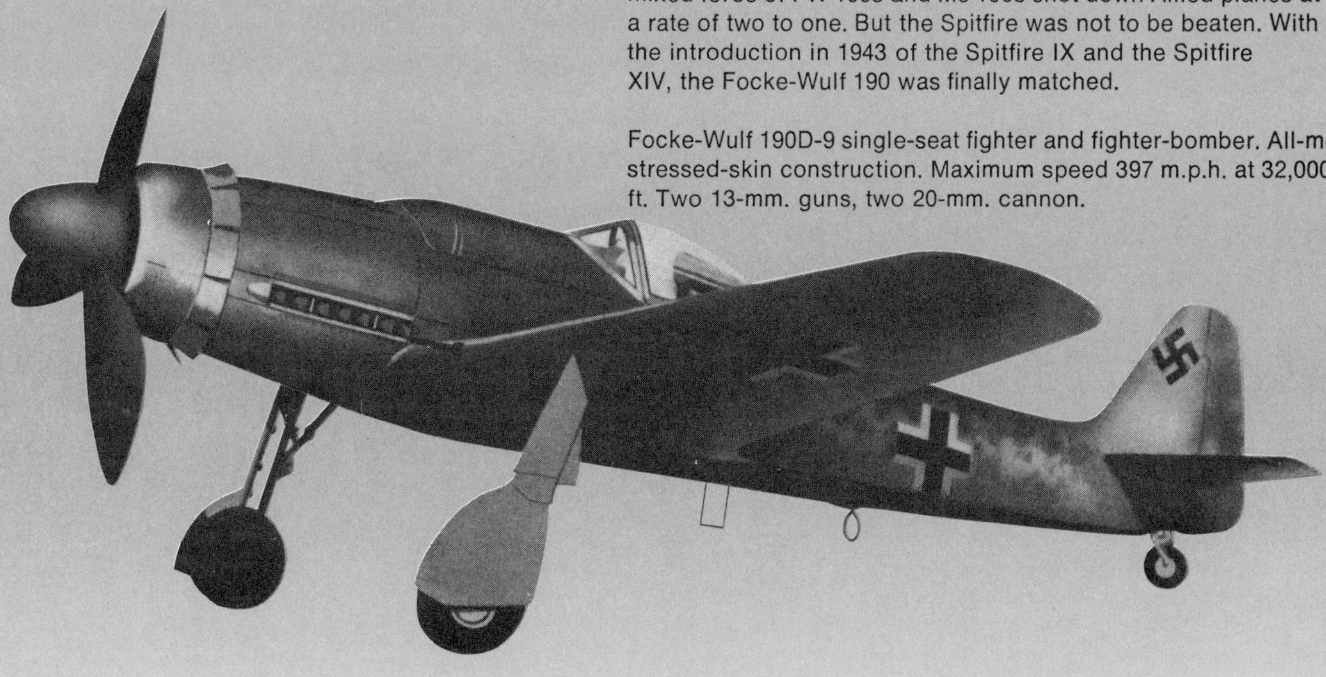

HAWKER TYPHOON

Four Canadian squadrons flew the Typhoon and from D-Day onward no plane was more deadly. Yet in its early days the Tiffy was almost abandoned as a "rogue" aircraft. Originally designed as a fighter-interceptor, it was rushed into action before it was fully cleared for service. The results were disastrous. Of the first 142 planes delivered, 135 had accidents due to engine or airframe failures. Proved inadequate as a high-altitude fighter, the Typhoon was saved by its thick, load-bearing wings. Armed with a 2000-pound bombload or eight 60-pound rocket missiles, it became one of war's hardest-hitting attack planes.

Hawker Typhoon single-seat fighter-bomber. All-metal stressed-skin construction. Maximum speed 404-413 m.p.h. depending on variant. Four 20-mm. cannon, but armament varied.

JUNKERS 87 (STUKA)

Swooping down in a near-vertical dive with its sirens howling, the vulture-like Junkers 87 dive-bomber was a terrifying weapon. In the blitzkrieg assaults on Poland and the Low Countries, it knocked out enemy positions with pinpoint accuracy. But in the Battle of Britain the Stuka at last met strong and determined fighter opposition and its weaknesses were swiftly revealed. Slow, ungainly and with only one gun to defend its stern, it was far from invincible. Severely routed, the Stuka was withdrawn from the battle and, although it continued to fight on other fronts, it never regained its reputation.

Junkers 87B dive-bomber (*Sturzkampfflugzeug*). All-metal stressed-skin construction. Maximum speed 217 m.p.h. at 16,000 ft. Three 7.9-mm. guns. Bombload 1500 lb.

DE HAVILLAND MOSQUITO

Night fighter, high-speed bomber, reconnaissance plane, ship-buster—the versatility of the two-engine Mosquito was unequaled. Built from wood—hence its nickname, the "termite's dream"—it combined great striking power with a speed that outpaced most German fighters. Its record was dazzling. Mosquito crews carried out many daring raids at rooftop height, made the first daylight bombing raid on Berlin, shot down scores of German bombers over Britain, blew up V-1 rocket sites, and torpedoed enemy ships. It was the fighter-bomber par excellence. More than 1000 were built in Canada.

De Havilland Mosquito (bomber variant). All-wood construction. Maximum speed (Mark IV) 380 m.p.h. at 17,000 ft. No defensive guns. Bombload 2000-4000 lb.

MESSERSCHMITT 110

Göring had high hopes for the Me 110. Named *Zerstörer* (Destroyer), its role was to fly escort to bombers and cut a path for them through enemy fighters. In the Battle of Britain Göring's dream was shattered. Pitted against Spitfires and Hurricanes, the two-engine fighter proved too unwieldy and sluggish and suffered heavy losses. A failure as a day escort, it redeemed itself as a night fighter. Equipped with radar, the Me 110 became a deadly hunter and shot down bombers by the hundreds in the RAF's great night offensive against Germany in 1943-44. It was also used as a fighter-bomber.

Messerschmitt 110C-4 two-seat fighter. All-metal stressed-skin construction. Maximum speed 349 m.p.h. at 22,900 ft. Five 7.9-mm. guns, two 20-mm. cannon.

GLOSTER METEOR

The Meteor was the RAF's first jet aircraft and the only Allied jet to see combat in World War II. Design work on the Meteor—originally called the Thunderbolt—began in 1940 and the first service models were delivered in 1944, just in time to go into action against the V-1 rocket missiles then being launched against England. Thirteen flying bombs were destroyed by Meteor pilots, two of them Canadians. The first Meteors to operate outside England arrived in Holland in April 1945, too late to challenge the German Me 262 jet fighter to a duel.

Gloster Meteor III single-seat fighter.
Two turbojet engines.
All-metal stressed-skin construction.
Maximum speed 493 m.p.h. at 30,000 ft.
Four 20-mm. cannon.

MESSERSCHMITT 262

The world's first operational jet plane, the Me 262 could have changed the course of the air war had it arrived earlier. Development began in 1938, but because the German air staff believed the war would last only one year the jet was given low priority. Hitler's absurd order to turn the 262 into a "blitz bomber" caused further delay and the fighter did not get into service until 1944. With a top speed of 540 m.p.h., it was far abler than any Allied plane and especially deadly when firing rocket missiles. But, of 1400 built, only 200 saw action—too few and too late to sway the battle.

Messerschmitt 262A single-seat fighter. Two turbojet engines. All-metal stressed-skin construction. Maximum speed 540 m.p.h. at 19,600 ft. Four 30-mm. cannon; some carried 24 50-mm. rocket missiles.

VICKERS WELLINGTON

Before the four-engine heavies took over, the faithful Wimpey was the backbone of Bomber Command and saw service with several Canadian squadrons. First flown in 1936, it had a rugged geodetic (lattice work) frame which could withstand heavy punishment from enemy flak. It flew on its first bombing raid on September 4, 1939, and was still going strong as a frontline bomber in Italy in March 1945. Wellingtons fought in all major theaters and were used in numerous roles including mine-laying and mine-clearing, radio counter-warfare, photo-reconnaissance, U-boat hunting and for troop transport and training operations.

Vickers Wellington IC two-engine medium bomber. Metal geodetic structure, fabric-covered. Maximum speed 235 m.p.h. at 15,500 ft. Six .303 guns. Bombload 4500 lb.

DORNIER 17

Called the Flying Pencil because of its long, slender fuselage, the Dornier 17 was one of three medium bombers used in Germany's early blitzkrieg campaigns. Starting life as a mail and passenger plane of the Lufthansa airline in 1934, it was redesigned in the following year as a high-speed bomber and first saw service in the Spanish civil war. Several hundred flew in the Battle of Britain but, although armed with six to eight machine guns, they were particularly vulnerable to stern attacks. The Dornier later served in the Balkans and on the Russian front but was withdrawn as a frontline bomber by the end of 1942.

Dornier 17Z medium bomber. All-metal stressed-skin construction. Maximum speed 265 m.p.h. at 16,400 ft. Six to eight 7.9-mm. guns. Bombload 2200 lb.

HANDLEY PAGE HALIFAX

The Champ, Big Chief Wa-Hoo, Vicky the Vicious Virgin—the names painted on Halifaxes by Canadian crews reflected the affection they felt for the big four-engine bombers which could take tremendous punishment and still get home. One called Friday the Thirteenth, skippered for a while by a Canadian, survived 128 sorties. First in action in 1941, the Halifax shared with the Lancaster the main burden of Bomber Command's offensive against Germany. It was also used to hunt U-boats, tow gliders on airborne operations and drop secret agents and arms to Resistance groups.

Halifax BIII heavy bomber. All-metal stressed-skin construction. Maximum speed 280 m.p.h. at 13,500 ft. Nine .303 guns. Bombload up to 13,000 lb.

JUNKERS 88

One of Germany's major blunders was her failure to build a long-range, four-engine bomber fleet. As a result the Luftwaffe had to rely on two-engine medium bombers. One of the best was the fast and sleek Junkers 88. Like the Mosquito, the Ju 88 was a remarkably versatile aircraft and was produced in many variants. In action on every German front, it served as both a dive and level bomber, torpedo bomber, minelayer, reconnaissance aircraft, day fighter and radar-equipped night fighter. The Ju 88 was first flown in 1936 and was still being produced in early 1945.

Junkers 88A-4 (bomber variant). All-metal stressed-skin construction. Maximum speed 247 m.p.h. at 14,000 ft. Seven 7.9-mm. guns, but armament varied. Bombload 5510 lb.

AVRO LANCASTER

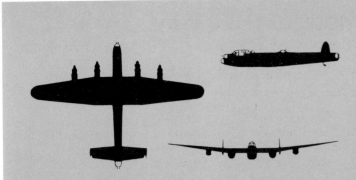

The four-engine Lancaster was the most successful bomber of the war. For all its size and power, it handled almost like a fighter. Said Canada's top bomber pilot, Johnnie Fauquier: "She flew as easily and as dexterously as a Tiger Moth. She had no bad habits." From mid-1942 on, the Lancaster flew on almost every major Bomber Command raid in Europe. It carried 14,000 pounds of bombs. Lancaster BI Specials of the famous Dambuster Squadron carried 22,000 pounds—more than even the American B29 Superfortress. Twelve RCAF squadrons flew Lancasters and more than 400 were built in Canada.

Avro Lancaster BI heavy bomber. All-metal stressed-skin construction. Maximum speed 275 m.p.h. at 15,000 ft. Nine .303 guns. Bombload 14-22,000 lb.

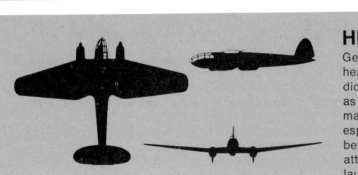

HEINKEL 111

Germany's standard level bomber, first flown in 1935, suffered heavy losses during the daylight raids of the Battle of Britain but did better in the night attacks that followed. Its chief drawback, as with other mediums, was its lack of range, which confined it mainly to tactical rather than strategic operations. This was especially so in Russia where many industrial plants were evacuated beyond bombing range. The He 111 was also used for torpedo attacks on Allied convoys to Russia. One of its last roles was to launch V-1 flying bombs against England. The rockets were released from an underwing carrier.

Heinkel 111H-5 medium bomber. All-metal stressed-skin construction. Maximum speed 240 m.p.h. at 14,000 ft. Seven 7.9-mm. guns. Bombload 5510 lb.

CONSOLIDATED CATALINA

The Catalina flying boat entered service with the U.S. Navy in 1936. During the war some 650 Catalinas were flown by the RAF and RCAF on anti-submarine patrols. One piloted by Sqdn. Ldr. Leonard Birchall saved Ceylon from surprise attack in April 1942 when Birchall sighted a Japanese fleet and radioed a warning before he was shot down. Flt. Lt. David Hornell, flying a version of the Catalina called the Canso, won the V.C. for a courageous attack on a U-boat and for his bravery when the crew had to ditch in the icy Atlantic. He died from exposure shortly after rescue.

Consolidated Catalina III (Canso A) flying boat. All-metal stressed-skin construction. Endurance 14 hours at 100 knots with 2000-lb. bombload (Mark I, 17 hours at 100 knots).

FOCKE-WULF 200 CONDOR

Another prewar German airliner converted to military use was the FW 200 which served the Luftwaffe as a long-range maritime patrol plane and bomber. Although the Condor made numerous successful attacks on ships—one victim was Canadian Pacific's *Empress of Britain,* which was set afire—the aircraft was too slow and unwieldy to be a true bomber and was also poorly armed. Its chief role was to find and shadow Atlantic convoys and direct U-boat wolf packs to them. Luckily for the Allies, Germany produced only 263 Condors, too few to be effective. One was used as Hitler's personal aircraft.

Focke-Wulf 200C-1 reconnaissance bomber. All-metal stressed-skin construction. Endurance 14 hours at 158 m.p.h. Three 13-mm. guns. Bombload 2150-3600 lb.

DOUGLAS DAKOTA

In a war so dependent on supplies, no aircraft was more vital than the Dakota, a military version of the prewar DC-3 airliner. The RCAF had three Dakota units. In Burma, 435 and 436 squadrons carried troops and supplies for the Fourteenth Army. Operating from jungle airstrips—sometimes under Japanese fire—they flew over some of the world's worst terrain, often in monsoon weather. In Europe, 437 Squadron participated in the great airborne landings at Grave, Eindhoven and Arnhem—flying, as one paratrooper put it, "straight into flaming hell." The squadron also took part in the airborne attack over the Rhine.

Douglas Dakota transport plane. All-metal stressed-skin construction. Maximum speed 230 m.p.h. at 8500 ft. Crew of three, 28 passengers. Maximum payload, 9000 lb.

JUNKERS 52

Nicknamed *Tante* (Auntie) by the Germans, the Junkers 52 tri-motor transport was a military version of a Lufthansa airliner flown in the early '30s. Tested as a bomber in Spain's civil war, it proved inadequate and served from then on as a transport and glider-tug plane. The Ju 52 flew on all German fronts. Some 500 took part in the famous airborne invasion of Crete in May 1941. More than 300 were used to ferry supplies to the Afrika Korps during Rommel's 1942 summer offensive, when they flew in 46,000 men and 4000 tons of supplies. Slow and poorly armed, the Ju 52 was easy prey for Allied fighters.

Junkers 52 transport plane. All-metal corrugated construction. Maximum speed 165 m.p.h. at sea level. One 13-mm., two 7.9-mm. guns. Two- or three-man crew and 18 passengers.

HOW A FIGHTER SQUADRON ATTACKED

A fighter squadron of the RCAF or RAF consisted usually of 12 aircraft operating in sections of three or four aircraft. Early in the war pilots were trained to fly in tight formation, each section in a disciplined V-shaped flight called a vic (A) or in line abreast (B) or line astern (C). Although good for flying discipline, close formations were easy for the enemy to spot and were also inferior tactically: the pilots had to divide their attention between keeping in position and watching for enemy planes.

Squadrons were also trained to engage enemy bombers in one of five standard attacks. For example, on the command "Attack number one—go!", the pilots swung behind their leader and followed him into attack in an orderly line, each firing as his turn came. These tactics proved disastrous and during the Battle of Britain were abandoned in favor of loose formations. Pilots now went into attack in elements of two: one leading and the other—called a wingman—guarding the leader's tail. Many squadrons later used a section formation called finger four (D) because the planes flew in positions similar to the fingertips of an outstretched hand. The section leader flew out front with his wingman flying on the side nearest the sun and looking down from the sun; the other pair was down sun of the leader and searched for enemy in the dangerous up-sun area. The planes flew about 200 yards apart and at different heights to cover one another better and scan a wider area. A tactic used by both sides was to dive on the enemy from out of the glare of the sun (E). The best and safest way to attack a fighter was from astern and above (F) because the target was not only easier to hit but could not return fire. A reflector sight (G) told the pilot when he was at the right distance to open fire. The sight's horizontal bars were moved in and out by a milled and numbered ring. If the pilot was attacking a Messerschmitt 109 he set the ring at 32—the length in feet of the Me 109's wingspan. When the enemy's silhouette filled the space between the bars, the pilot knew he was in firing range.

The gyroscopic sight (H), introduced later, not only gave the range but also calculated how much lead or deflection was needed so that the bullets would hit an enemy plane flying at an angle or across in front (I). The pilot flew his plane so that the target was between a pair of diamonds.

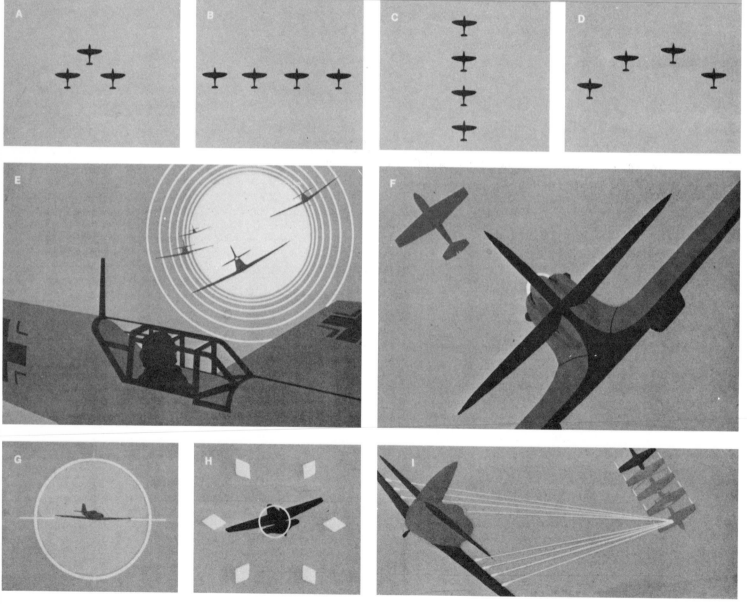

HOW BOMBER CREWS FOUND TARGETS AT NIGHT

1 Before radar aids came, RAF navigators found their way by taking fixes on landmarks or stars—an almost impossible job on cloudy nights and in heavy winds. Says an official history: "What is surprising is not that so many crews failed to find the target but that more did not fail to find England on return." 2 Germans raiding Britain used Lorenz radio beams directed at the target from ground transmitters. The pilot kept on course by listening to a steady note through the earphones of a radio receiver; if he strayed right or left he heard dots or dashes. 3 Oboe radar, introduced by the RAF in 1942, used radio beams from two ground stations. One, Cat, guided the bomber along an arc to the target. Mouse calculated the point on the arc at which the bombs should be dropped, and radioed a "bomb release" signal. 4 To detect bombers, the Germans set up a chain of early-warning radar posts. Each had three radars. Freya (A) picked up a bomber 75 miles away. Defenses were alerted and a night fighter sent to orbit the

station. As the bomber closed, a Würzburg radar (B) tracked it. A similar set (C) guided the fighter until its own radar (D) could home on the bomber. 5 From July 1943 on, the bombers jammed German radar by dropping thousands of metal foil strips called Window, producing a mass of confusing blips on enemy radar screens. 6 The Germans countered by equipping night fighters with radar impervious to Window. To thwart this, RAF planes with special jamming gear were sent ahead of the main force to blot out German radar transmissions. Circling in pairs, they formed a screen to shield the bomber's approach. 7 H2S radar, introduced by the RAF in 1943, helped a navigator "see" through the dark and fix his position. The radar bounced echoes off the ground, producing a map-like pattern of the area below on a cathode ray tube screen (A). Rivers, lakes and towns produced distinctive echo patterns, enabling the navigator to "map-read" his way to the target (B).

THE BOMBER CREW

When RAF Bomber Command had only two-engine planes, the normal bomber crew numbered six: pilot, co-pilot, wireless operator, two air gunners and an overworked observer who acted as navigator, bomb-aimer and gunner. In 1942, as four-engine planes came into service, the crew was reorganized. The co-pilot was replaced by a flight engineer, a specialist bomb-aimer was introduced and the observer, renamed navigator, was responsible only for navigation. The Lancaster's seven-man crew, left to right: bomb-aimer, who also manned the front gun; pilot, on left side of plane, with flight engineer on his right; navigator, wireless operator, mid-upper gunner, rear gunner. Pathfinding Lancasters usually carried two navigators, one being an H2S radar operator and bomb-aimer. The radar scanner was housed in an underbelly dome as shown. The RAF's No. 100 Group Lancasters had an extra man to operate radio-jamming gear or other radar counter-warfare equipment.

THE BOMBS THEY DROPPED

Bomber Command used three main types of bomb: target indicator, incendiary and high-explosive. Target indicators were colorful fireworks bombs set to explode either in the sky or on the ground to mark the bomb-release point. Incendiaries were small four-pound magnesium fire bombs stowed in clusters inside a large cylindrical container which opened at 2000 feet and scattered the bombs over the target. Of the high explosives, the most common were GP (general purpose) bombs, weighing 250 and 500 pounds. Far larger and more devastating were the high-blast blockbusters which ranged from 2000 to 12,000 pounds. These were thin steel cylinders filled with Amatol and TNT explosives, which composed up to 80% of a bomb's total weight. In the latter part of the war, Dr. Barnes Wallis, inventor of the dambuster bomb, produced two other huge missiles: the 12,000-pound Tallboy and 22,000-pound Grand Slam deep-penetration bombs. They were used successfully against the German battleship *Tirpitz,* to blow up viaducts, and to destroy the German Navy's U-boat pens. Here, from left to right, are some of the bombs: 4000-pound blockbuster; 100-pound anti-submarine bomb; 500-pound GP bomb; 2000-pound armor-piercing bomb; 600-pound anti-submarine bomb; 1000-pound medium capacity bomb; 500-pound incendiary cluster containing 106 four-pound magnesium fire bombs; the 12,000-pound Tallboy and 22,000-pound Grand Slam deep-penetration bombs.

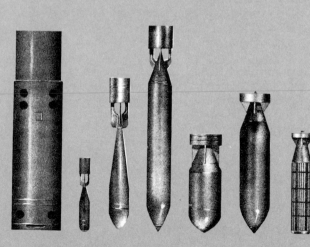

HITLER'S SECRET WEAPONS

Hitler called them his *Vergeltungswaffen* (reprisal weapons)—the long-range rocket bombs he hoped would win him the war. They might have, too, but the Allies discovered their secret base at Peenemünde and bombed it in August 1943, delaying rocket production during the crucial year of the buildup for the Normandy invasion.

The first V-1 flying bombs (left) were fired June 13, 1944, a week after D-Day. They were launched against England from ramps in France and Holland or released from aircraft over the North Sea. A V-1 was driven by a pulse jet engine (A) and steered on a preset course by an automatic pilot (B) which was powered by compressed air in bottles (C). This air also drove the controls (D) operating the rudder and elevators; and it forced fuel from the 130-gallon tank (E) into the jet motor. The fuses and one-ton warhead (F) were in the nose section, and at the tip was a small windmill (G). This turned a mileage counter which activated the elevators to send the bomb into a steep dive when it reached the target area.

V-2 ROCKET BOMBS

Far more sophisticated—and more accurate and deadly—were the V-2 rocket missiles. Launched from mobile pads in Holland, they hurtled silently through space at 3500 m.p.h. —almost ten times the speed of the V-1s. On long-range firing against targets in England, the V-2 trajectory reached a height of 50 to 60 miles. The fuses and one-ton warhead were in the nose (A). Then came the guidance controls (B) and tanks of alcohol (C) and liquid oxygen (D) which were fed by pump (E) into the combustion chamber (F) and burned. The V-2's total weight was 13 tons. Once full-scale production was ordered, the time taken to complete a bomb dropped

from 19,000 man-hours in 1943 to 4000 in early 1945.

The V-1 flying bombs, called doodlebugs by the British, could be shot down by fighter planes and anti-aircraft guns, and of some 8000 launched against London and southern England only 2400 got through the defenses. But there was no defense against the V-2 rockets except to try to bomb the launching sites—which the Germans constantly moved to avoid detection. The first V-2 was fired in September 1944. Before the First Canadian Army overran Holland in April 1945 some 5000 V-2s had been launched. They killed 11,000 persons.

THE MEN

He was about 18 when he joined the navy and chances are he'd never seen the sea. The process of turning him into a sailor often began far inland. Then he was sent to Esquimalt, B.C., or Halifax or, after May 1942, HMCS *Cornwallis,* near Digby, N.S. Whether his specialty was gunnery, communications, radar, asdic or the engine room, he learned at sea to fight the elements as well as the enemy. His shipboard uniform was mostly foul-weather gear. He worked in watches: four hours on and, if he was lucky, eight off. Sometimes it was four-on-four-off for days on end. As an able seaman he was paid $1.85 a day.

A handful were career soldiers and some had been in militia units, but most World War II Canadian soldiers went directly from farm, factory or office —or from the ranks of the unemployed— to sign up for the private's $1.30 a day. The private's rifle was the Lee Enfield, a modern version of the basic weapon his father had used in World War I. His steel helmet was like the 1914-18 model too but covered with a camouflage net. His battle kit included an anti-gas respirator in a haversack, a packsack, a ground sheet, an entrenching tool, hand grenades and pouches for rifle and Bren-gun ammunition.

The RCAF recruit first became an AC2 (aircraftsman second class). If chosen for aircrew he went to an elementary flying school, then took advanced training which led to graduation, wings and promotion to sergeant pilot (above). After more courses and time in an operational training unit, he was posted to an operational squadron. His pay was $3.70 a day, including aircrew allowance, and his prospects of promotion to pilot officer were excellent. This sergeant wears a flying helmet and goggles, life belt, flight boots and oxygen mask. He carries a jack to plug into his fighter plane radio. Canada trained almost 50,000 pilots.

THE RANKS: NAVY, ARMY, AIR FORCE

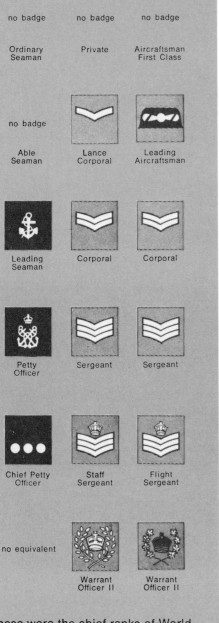

Navy	Army	Air Force
no badge — Ordinary Seaman	no badge — Private	no badge — Aircraftsman First Class
no badge — Able Seaman	Lance Corporal	Leading Aircraftsman
Leading Seaman	Corporal	Corporal
Petty Officer	Sergeant	Sergeant
Chief Petty Officer	Staff Sergeant	Flight Sergeant
no equivalent	Warrant Officer II	Warrant Officer II

Navy	Army	Air Force
no equivalent	Warrant Officer I	Warrant Officer I
Acting Sub Lieutenant	Second Lieutenant	Pilot Officer
Sub Lieutenant	Lieutenant	Flying Officer
Lieutenant	Captain	Flight Lieutenant
Lieutenant Commander	Major	Squadron Leader
Commander	Lieutenant Colonel	Wing Commander

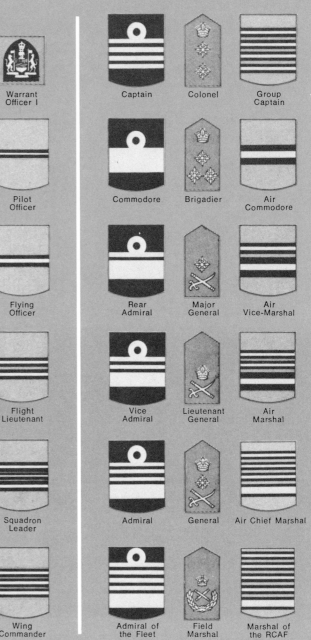

Navy	Army	Air Force
Captain	Colonel	Group Captain
Commodore	Brigadier	Air Commodore
Rear Admiral	Major General	Air Vice-Marshal
Vice Admiral	Lieutenant General	Air Marshal
Admiral	General	Air Chief Marshal
Admiral of the Fleet	Field Marshal	Marshal of the RCAF

These were the chief ranks of World War II, many destined to be discarded in the late 1960s when the navy, army and air force became the Canadian Armed Forces. Naval and air force officers wore their rank on their sleeves; army officers' rank was on the shoulder straps. All three services wore battledress, with rank on the shoulders. Most NCO ranks were worn above the elbow but naval chief petty officers and RCAF and army warrant officers wore theirs just above the cuff. Top wartime Canadian ranks were vice-admiral, general and air marshal.

THE DECORATIONS

The Victoria Cross is the highest decoration a Canadian serviceman could win for valor in the presence of the enemy. It was instituted in 1856. The next highest, the George Cross, is for gallantry *not* in the presence of the enemy. It may be awarded to civilians. Other principal decorations and awards for bravery in action:

Distinguished Service Order—officers of all services and the merchant service; Distinguished Service Cross—naval officers, lieutenant commander and below; Military Cross—army officers, majors and below; Distinguished Flying Cross—air force officers; Air Force Cross—officers and civilians;

Distinguished Conduct Medal—army warrant officers and below; Conspicuous Gallantry Medal—navy chief petty officers and below; Conspicuous Gallantry Medal (Flying)—warrant officers and below;

George Medal—for bravery not considered equal to that for which the George Cross is awarded;

Distinguished Service Medal—navy petty officers and below; Military Medal—army warrant officers and below; Distinguished Flying Medal—air force NCOs and men; Air Force Medal—warrant officers and below, and civilians.

Tweedsmuir (signature)

Canada

GEORGE THE SIXTH, by the Grace of God of Great Britain, Ireland and the British Dominions beyond the Seas KING, Defender of the Faith, Emperor of India.

TO ALL TO WHOM these Presents shall come or whom the same may in anywise concern,

GREETING:---

Ernest Lapointe (signature)

ATTORNEY GENERAL,
CANADA.

A PROCLAMATION.

WHEREAS by and with the advice of Our Privy Council for Canada We have Signified Our Approval of the issue of a Proclamation in the "Canada Gazette" declaring that a State of War with the German Reich exists and has existed in Our Dominion of Canada as and from the *tenth* day of September, 1939;

NOW THEREFORE We Do Hereby Declare and Proclaim that a State of War with the German Reich exists and has existed in Our Dominion of Canada as and from the *tenth* day of September, 1939.

OF ALL WHICH Our Loving Subjects and all others whom these Presents may concern are hereby required to take notice and to govern themselves accordingly.

IN TESTIMONY WHEREOF We have caused these Our Letters to be made Patent and the Great Seal of Canada to be hereunto affixed.

WITNESS:---Our Right Trusty and Well-beloved John, Baron Tweedsmuir of Elsfield, a Member of Our Most Honourable Privy Council, Knight Grand Cross of Our Most Distinguished Order of Saint Michael and Saint George, Knight Grand Cross of Our Royal Victorian Order, Member of Our Order of the Companions of Honour, Governor General and Commander-in-Chief of Our Dominion of Canada.

AT OUR GOVERNMENT HOUSE, in Our City of Ottawa, this *tenth* day of September in the year of Our Lord One thousand nine hundred and thirty-nine and in the Third year of Our Reign.

BY COMMAND,

W. L. Mackenzie King. (signature)

PRIME MINISTER OF CANADA.

Diary of a War

1939

September

1—Germans invade Poland in first Nazi blitzkrieg.

3—Britain and France declare war on Germany. Liner *Athenia* torpedoed en route to Montreal.

8—Parliament meets. Prime Minister Mackenzie King says conscription out, stresses buildup of navy, air force, munitions-making.

0—Canada for the first time makes her own declaration of war.

6—First convoy leaves Halifax.

7—Russians invade Poland under secret understanding with Germany.

4—Premier Duplessis calls Quebec election for October 25, declaring a vote for him is "a vote for autonomy against conscription."

6—Britain proposes Canada train Commonwealth airmen.

7—Poland surrenders, is soon partitioned by Germany and Russia.

October

5—Maj. Gen. A. G. L. McNaughton named to head 1st Division.

4—British battleship *Royal Oak* torpedoed and sunk at Scapa Flow naval base.

5—Duplessis government beaten by Liberals in Quebec election, removing threat to war effort.

November

1—Trans-Canada Air Lines starts daily coast-to-coast flights.

0—Russia invades Finland.

December

1—Finance Minister J. L. Ralston says Canada's war effort should be "practical rather than spectacular."

3—German pocket battleship *Graf Spee* driven into neutral harbor at Montevideo, Uruguay, by British warships.

7—First elements of 1st Division arrive in Britain. British Commonwealth Air Training Plan Agreement signed at Ottawa. Germans scuttle *Graf Spee* off Montevideo.

8—In war's biggest air battle to date, 12 German and 12 British planes lost over Heligoland and in sea.

Battleship escorting 1st Canadian Division to Britain —December 1939

1940

January

18—Ontario Legislature condemns war effort as inadequate.

25—Federal election called on heels of Ontario resolution.

February

11—Governor-General Lord Tweedsmuir dies.

16—RCAF's No. 110 Army Cooperation Squadron sails for Britain—first of 48 squadrons to go overseas.

17—British destroyers raid German ship *Altmark* in Norwegian fjord and free 299 British prisoners.

March

12—Russian-Finnish war ends. Finland cedes territory.

26—Mackenzie King's Liberal government re-elected.

28—Cabinet approves choice of Earl of Athlone as Governor-General.

April

9—Germany invades Denmark and Norway. Denmark offers no resistance; Norway fights. After heavy losses, RAF abandons daylight bombing for night raids.

9-13—British sink 3 German cruisers, 10 destroyers in Norway.

25—Two Canadian battalions slated to join British force bound for Norway are halted in Scotland.

May

2—British withdrawing from Norway.

3—Norwegian Army surrenders. Vidkun Quisling heads pro-German government.

10—Germany invades Holland, Belgium, Luxembourg. Britain's Prime Minister Chamberlain resigns. Winston Churchill takes over.

11—Churchill names Canadian-born Lord Beaverbrook minister of aircraft production.

THE EVENING TELEGRAM

CHURCHILL NEW PREMIER

German Surprise Attack Has Been Foiled, Declare Dutch
Defenders Trap Parachute Troops—Nazis Lose 70 Planes

BRITAIN ON WATCH FOR INVASION BY AIR

14—Holland capitulates.

17—British begin strategic withdrawal on western front.

20—Germans thrust to English Channel.

22—C. G. Power named air minister in Ottawa.

24—Four Canadian destroyers answer Britain's call for help.

26—Evacuation of British, other troops through Dunkirk begins.

28—Belgium surrenders.

29—Canadian Parliament passes $700 million war appropriations bill. Whole war effort stepped up. Two more divisions authorized.

June

4—Dunkirk evacuation completed; 340,000 Allied troops get to Britain. RAF's 242 "Canadian" Squadron posted to France. Churchill says Britain and Commonwealth will fight on alone if necessary.

5—Canada declares 16 Nazi, Fascist, Communist organizations illegal.

8—British aircraft carrier *Glorious* lost with 1200 lives. RCAF's No. 1 Fighter Squadron sails for Britain.

10—Italy declares war on Britain, France. Canada at war with Italy. Defense Minister Norman Rogers killed in air crash.

13—J. L. Ralston becomes defense minister. Canadian brigade leaves Britain to try to form defense line across France's Brittany peninsula.

14—Undefended Paris falls to Germans.

15-16—Canadians withdraw from France. Russians occupy Latvia, Estonia, Lithuania.

18—Canada announces obligatory military training for home defense. Canadian forces now in Britain, Iceland, Newfoundland and West Indies. RAF's 242 "Canadian" Squadron withdraws from France. Churchill warns Battle of Britain coming.

19—Britain organizes to evacuate children to Canada. Ottawa considering steps to be taken if Royal Navy withdraws to Canada.

22—France signs humiliating armistice. Canada becomes Britain's chief ally.

25—Canadian destroyer *Fraser* sunk in collision off France.

July

2—Liner *Arandora Star* torpedoed en route to Canada. Survivors rescued by destroyer *St. Laurent*.

3—King and Queen reject suggestions to send two princesses to Canada. Royal Navy seizes French battleship in British port, sinks battleship and aircraft carrier at Oran, North Africa.

8—Nova Scotia's Premier Angus L. Macdonald becomes navy minister.

9—France becomes corporative state under Pétain, with capital at Vichy.

Allied soldiers captured at Dunkirk—June 10, 1940

—Luftwaffe hammers shipping, harbors as Battle of Britain begins.

—PO. D. A. Hewitt is first Canadian killed in Battle of Britain.

—Anglo-Canadian 7th Corps comes into existence, commanded by Canada's A. G. L. McNaughton, promoted to lieutenant general.

ugust

1—Part of 2nd Canadian Division reaches Britain.

2—Montreal's Mayor Camillien Houde attacks national registration for home defense.

5—Houde interned. Italians invade Somaliland in Africa.

3—Luftwaffe switches attacks to British airfields, factories.

5—Sqdn. Ldr. Ernest McNab scores first RCAF kill in Battle of Britain.

7—RCAF's No. 1 Fighter Squadron in action.

8—President Roosevelt, Prime Minister King announce U.S.-Canadian joint defense board.

19—British evacuate Somaliland.

28—U.S. Senate passes conscription bill.

30—RAF's "Canadian" Squadron in action in Battle of Britain.

September

3—Britain gives neutral U.S. military bases in West Indies, Newfoundland, gets 50 overage destroyers of which 7 go to Canada.

7—Luftwaffe starts blitz of London.

13—Italians advance into Egypt.

15—Turning point in Battle of Britain. RAF claims 183 planes destroyed, a figure later cut to 56.

17—Hitler postpones indefinitely his plans for invasion of Britain.

25—Canadian armed merchantman *Prince Robert* captures German ship *Weser* in Pacific off Mexico.

27—Japan joins the Rome-Berlin Axis for mutual defense.

October

7—Germans enter Romania to "guard" oil fields.

23—Canadian destroyer *Margaree* sunk in Atlantic collision.

26—Canadian Pacific liner *Empress of Britain,* bombed two days earlier, is torpedoed and sunk in Atlantic.

28—Italians invade Greece.

November

1—Greeks report Italians repulsed everywhere.

3—Commonwealth troops land to help Greeks.

5—British armed merchant cruiser *Jervis Bay* goes down fighting German raider in Atlantic, allows convoy to escape. Franklin Roosevelt elected U.S. President for third time.

10—Canada, Britain start bomber air ferry service across Atlantic.

11—British smash Italian fleet at Taranto.

14—German air raid devastates Coventry, England.

20—Hungary joins Axis powers.

24—First Canadian graduates of air training plan reach Britain.

December

5—Destroyer *Saguenay,* first Canadian warship torpedoed, limps to British port. First corvettes have joined Battle of Atlantic.

18—Munitions Minister C. D. Howe and 152 other survivors of torpedoed liner *Western Prince* arrive in Britain.

25—Two-division Canadian Corps established in Britain.

29—Worst night of London blitz.

1941

January

5—Italians surrender Libyan port of Bardia to Australians and British.

8—Ottawa orders registration of Japanese Canadians in British Columbia.

20—London announces 23,081 killed in German air attacks on England.

22—Australians complete capture of Tobruk in Libya, taking 25,000 Italians prisoner.

29—British invade Somaliland in widening African offensive against Italians.

31—British whip Italians at Agordat in Eritrea.

February

3—Canada extends compulsory military training from one month to four.

6—Australians enter Benghazi.

7—British complete capture of Benghazi, climaxing audacious 62-day campaign that destroyed 10 Italian divisions.

12—German troops in Africa to bolster Italians.

21—On war mission, Nobel Prize winner Sir Frederick Banting killed in Newfoundland air crash.

March

4—British sink 11 enemy ships in surprise raid on Norway's Lofoten Islands.

11—U.S. Congress approves Lend-Lease, opening way for all-out aid to Britain.

26—Yugoslav government is overthrown by pro-Allied regime.

27—Keren falls to British, breaking Italian resistance in Eritrea.

28—British sink five Italian warships off Cape Matapan, gain supremacy in Mediterranean.

29—British occupy Diredawa, Ethiopia.

30—Germany's Rommel launches counteroffensive in Cyrenaica, Africa.

April

1—Two German ships scuttled off Peru when intercepted by Canadian armed merchant cruiser *Prince Henry.*

6—British enter Addis Ababa, Ethiopian capital, and now control virtually all Italian East Africa. Germans attack Yugoslavia and Greece.

8—Greeks abandon Salonika.

13—Axis forces take Bardia, Libya. Tobruk holds out. Long siege begins.

15—No. 402 Fighter Squadron makes RCAF's first attack over enemy territory.

17—Yugoslav Army surrenders but guerrilla resistance continues. British land in Iraq to guard oil fields.

20—In Hyde Park Declaration, Roosevelt and King pool North America's industrial resources.

24—Greece surrenders. British forces withdrawing.

30—Canadian passenger ship *Nerissa* torpedoed off Ireland; 73 Canadian Army personnel lost.

May

10—Rudolf Hess, No. 2 Nazi, parachutes into Scotland on personal peace mission. Britain's House of Commons destroyed by bombs.

20—German airborne attack on British-held Crete, Mediterranean island.

22—British lose six warships off Crete.

24—British battleship *Hood* sunk by German battleship *Bismarck* in Atlantic.

27—*Bismarck* caught, sunk by planes, warships.

31—British evacuate Crete.

June

8—British and Free French attack Syria. Vichy French fight back.

12—First RCAF bombing attack on Germany.

13—Canada's Commodore L. W. Murray heads new escort force based on Newfoundland. Northwest Atlantic Canada's responsibility.

15—British in Libyan offensive toward Tobruk.

22—Germany attacks Russia from Black Sea to Baltic. Italy, Romania, Finland at war with Russia. Churchill promises Russia help.

28—Russians forced back to old Russian-Polish frontier.

July

2—RCAF authorized to enlist women, followed by army, navy.

3—Stalin urges Russians to adopt "scorched earth" policy, guerrilla warfare.

7—U.S. puts troops into Iceland, sharing British occupation.

Germans retreat from Moscow—December 1941

14—Allies occupy Vichy French Syria and Lebanon.

16—Germans in Russia reach Smolensk.

24—Japan moves into French Indo-China (Viet Nam) with Vichy French approval.

26—Roosevelt halts U.S. trade with Japan.

August

2—Germans drive into Ukraine.

9—Churchill and Roosevelt meet at sea off Newfoundland.

12—Eight-point Atlantic Charter of war aims signed by Churchill and Roosevelt.

23—Prime Minister Mackenzie King booed by restless Canadian troops in England.

25—British and Russians invade Iran. Canadian troops land in Norwegian island of Spitsbergen, destroy anything of use to Germans.

September

8—Germans encircle Leningrad.

10—Canadian corvettes sink first submarine.

11—Angered by U-boat attacks on U.S. ships, Roosevelt orders U.S. Navy to "shoot on sight" at Axis planes, ships.

19—Germans capture Kiev, capital of Ukraine, isolate Crimea. Canadian corvette *Levis* torpedoed.

October

16—Panic in Moscow as Germans approach. Government flees to Kubyshev. Russians abandon Odessa. U.S. destroyer *Kearney* sunk by Germans.

17—Militant Gen. Hideki Tojo forms new Japanese government.

18—Mackenzie King announces ceiling on Canadian wages, prices in move to combat inflation.

25—Germans take Kharkov, Ukraine industrial center. RCAF's Eastern Command makes first attack on submarine off Newfoundland.

27—Canadian Army force, 1975 strong, sails for Hong Kong to reinforce garrison.

29—Germans push into Crimea.

31—U.S. destroyer *Reuben James* torpedoed and sunk in Atlantic.

November

10—Britain warns she will declare war if Japan strikes in Pacific.

13—British battleship *Ark Royal* sunk.

16—Tojo claims Japan being economically blockaded by methods "little short of war."

18—British Eighth Army begins offensive in Libya.

26—U.S.-Japanese talks reach critical point in Washington. Japanese are told to get out of China, Indo-China. Canada's Justice Minister

Ernest Lapointe dies in hospital in Montreal.

0—Russians drive Germans from Rostov-on-Don.

ecember

5—Germans abandon Moscow offensive for winter.

6—Russians counterattack before Moscow.

7—Japan attacks U.S. Pacific naval base at Pearl Harbor. Canadian corvette *Windflower* lost in Atlantic collision.

8—Japanese attack Hong Kong, Thailand, Malaya, the Philippines. Allies declare war on Japan. Russia remains neutral.

9—Blackouts ordered on Canada's west coast. Japanese-Canadian newspapers, schools closed. Fears of invasion spread. Tobruk garrison relieved by Eighth Army in Africa.

0—British battleship *Prince of Wales*, battle cruiser *Repulse* sunk by Japanese air attacks off coast of Malaya. In Ottawa, Louis St. Laurent

is sworn in as minister of justice, succeeding Ernest Lapointe.

11—Japanese repulsed by Americans at Wake Island.

12—Germans routed before Moscow, retreat in bitter weather.

18—Japanese troops cross from Kowloon to attack Hong Kong island. Canadians heavily involved in fighting. British report Axis forces driven back in full flight in Libya.

22—Churchill arrives in Washington for conference with Roosevelt.

23—Japanese capture Wake Island.

25—Hong Kong surrenders. Canadian dead include CSM. J. R. Osborn, later awarded V.C.

30—Churchill addresses Canadian Parliament.

31—RCAF has 14 squadrons operating overseas, 7 more authorized, plus 16 at home, including 8 on west coast. RCN has 64 corvettes fighting Battle of Atlantic. Army concentrating in Britain for invasion of Europe.

1942

January

1—Twenty-six countries sign Declaration of the United Nations, forming a great coalition against the Axis.

2—Japanese enter Manila, capital of Philippines. Gen. Douglas MacAr-

thur's army retreats to Bataan peninsula for heroic stand. Eighth Army storms Bardia, Libya. Canada decides to make $1 billion gift of war supplies to Britain.

11—Japanese invade Netherlands East Indies and sweep British down Malayan peninsula, capturing Kuala Lumpur.

14—British Columbia coastal region defined as "protected area." Japanese aliens ordered out.

16—Japanese invade Burma.

19—Canadian ship *Lady Hawkins* torpedoed as U-boats ravage unprotected shipping along Atlantic coast of North America.

23—Japanese landing in Solomon Islands.

29—Axis forces, in Libyan counteroffensive, capture Benghazi.

February

9—Former Prime Minister Arthur Meighen, pro-conscription Conservative leader, defeated in Toronto by-election, losing bid for Commons seat.

10—Canadian corvette *Spikenard* torpedoed.

12—German battle cruisers *Scharnhorst, Gneisenau* leave Brest, France, escape to north despite air attacks in which nine Canadian squadrons lose seven planes.

15—British surrender Singapore.

26—Japanese Canadians ordered evacuated from west coast.

28—Enemy air attacks raging against Malta, British threat to Axis domination of Mediterranean.

March

8—Rangoon falls to Japanese.

9—Allied forces surrender in Netherlands East Indies.

17—Gen. Douglas MacArthur lands in Australia to take charge of fight against Japan.

18—Single military commands established over Canadian forces in Atlantic, Newfoundland, Pacific areas. Alcan (Alaska) Highway under construction.

Japanese marines occupy Kiska
—June 6-7, 1942

24—Ottawa announces selective service program for industry, meets manpower shortage by directing people to jobs.

April

4—RCAF's Sqdn. Ldr. L. J. Birchall spots Japanese fleet heading for Ceylon naval base, averts second Pearl Harbor.

5—Attack on Ceylon beaten off as tide of Japanese conquest reaches western limits.

6—First Canadian Army, under Gen.

A. G. L. McNaughton, formed in Britain with five divisions, two armored brigades. Three other divisions slated for home defense.

9—Americans surrender in Philippines' Bataan peninsula.

13—RCAF's 417 Fighter Squadron heads for Egypt to join Desert Air Force.

18—U.S. Army planes, under Col. James H. Doolittle, bomb Tokyo.

27—National plebiscite gives Ottawa power to impose overseas conscription "if necessary." But French-speaking Quebec votes a resounding "no."

29—Japanese capture Lashio, terminus of Burma Road, supply route to Chinese armies tying down one third of Japanese strength. Capture completes conquest of central Burma.

May

1—British evacuate Mandalay, Burma.

4-8—Both Americans, Japanese claim victory in Battle of Coral Sea.

6—Final surrender of U.S.-Filipino forces in Philippines.

11—British steamer sunk in Gulf as Battle of St. Lawrence begins. Works Minister P. J. A. Cardin re-

signs from federal cabinet ov conscription issue.

13—Ottawa announces two ships lc in St. Lawrence.

19—Germans, after winter retreats, offensive in Crimea.

20—All Burma in Japanese hands. Br ish withdraw into India. Chine being supplied by air.

26—Afrika Korps attacks in Libya.

30—RAF's first thousand-plane bomb raid ravages Germany's Cologn More than 500 Canadians involve

June

3-6—Japanese lose heavily in great ai and sea Battle of Midway.

6-7—Japanese land in Alaskan islanc of Kiska, Attu.

9—Sgt. George "Buzz" Beurlir reaches Malta, begins meteor rise to top rank among Canadia fighter pilots.

10—Germans butcher Czech village Lidice in reprisal for slaying of N zi official.

16—British lose 5 warships, 30 plane sink Italian cruiser, damage 8 oth warships, down 65 Axis planes four-day Mediterranean convc battle as attempts to succor Malt go on.

20—Isolated Estevan Point on Vanco ver Island shelled by Japanes submarine.

21—Rommel's Afrika Korps capture key Tobruk, takes 25,000 priso ers, pushes eastward into Egyp

July

1—Sevastopol, main Russian strong hold on Black Sea, falls to Ge mans, Romanians after 25-da siege.

2—British halt Rommel at El Alamei Egypt.

13—Ottawa announces three mor sinkings in St. Lawrence. Outcr rises in Quebec for protectio soon forces secret Commons se sion.

23—Germans capture Rostov-on-Don.

August

3—Corvette *Sackville* sinks sub in A lantic, one of four destroyed b RCN in five weeks.

7—U.S. marines land on Guadalcana Solomon Islands.

13—Gen. Bernard Montgomery take over Eighth Army in Egypt.

15—Gen. Sir Harold Alexander be comes Middle East commander.

German infantry and armor in the Caucasus—summer, 1942

19—Canadians suffer heavy losses, win two Victoria Crosses in nine-hour raid on Dieppe.

27—RCN corvette *Oakville* sinks sub in Caribbean as part of fight to keep oil moving to Britain. German sub sinks two ships off Newfoundland.

September

6—Germans halted at Stalingrad.

11—Canadian corvette *Charlottetown* lost in Gulf of St. Lawrence less than a week after loss of patrol vessel *Raccoon*.

13—Destroyer *Ottawa* torpedoed as Battle of Atlantic moves toward its greatest period of crisis.

18—Germans cut off Crimea, take city of Kiev.

20—Australians halt Japanese drive on Port Moresby, New Guinea.

21—Violent street fighting in Stalingrad.

25—Sqdn. Ldr. K. A. Boomer destroys Japanese fighter off Alaska in RCAF's only air combat in North American theater.

October

4—Stalin calls on Allies to open second front.

14—U-boat torpedoes Canadian steamship *Caribou* in Cabot Strait, 136 lost. Battle of St. Lawrence ends after taking 700 lives, 23 ships. Buzz Beurling is wounded and shot down in Malta.

23—Montgomery's Eighth Army attacks at El Alamein.

30—RCAF planes of Eastern Air Command destroy two subs in one day.

November

4—Start of Afrika Korps retreat from El Alamein.

8—Allies, in first major invasion, land in Algeria and French Morocco, North Africa, with Canadian warships among supporting naval formations.

11—Germans invade unoccupied part of France.

13—Eighth Army retakes Tobruk.

18—Guy Bieler becomes first Canadian Army secret agent to parachute into France.

19—Russians launch counterattack at besieged Stalingrad.

20—Eighth Army takes Benghazi.

27—French scuttle their battle fleet at Toulon as Germans approach.

December

2—Mackenzie King proposes new world order based on human rights and universal rule of law. Canadian bomber crew, British scientist badly shot up but their secret mission gets key information on German airborne radar, a necessary prelude to major bomber offensive. In Chicago, world's first nuclear chain reaction opens atomic age.

21—Butter rationing starts in Canada.

26-30—Canadian-escorted convoy ONS-154 loses 14 ships but gets 32 to Britain. Battle of Atlantic at peak with U-boat forces doubled in one year.

1943

January

1—Canada's largest air formation, No. 6 Bomber Group, begins operations from England. RCAF now has 31 squadrons overseas, 36 more at home.

6—Germans retreat from Caucasus.

13—Corvette *Ville de Québec* makes Canada's first U-boat kill in Mediterranean.

14-24—Roosevelt, Churchill meet at Casablanca, call for Germany's "unconditional surrender."

23—Eighth Army occupies Tripoli, drives Axis forces into Tunisia.

27—After appalling losses, Germans establish line far west of Stalingrad.

30—Submarine expert Adm. Karl Dönitz takes over command of German Navy.

February

2—Germans surrender after long siege of Stalingrad.

6—Canadian corvette *Louisburg* torpedoed in Mediterranean.

7—Japanese evacuate Guadalcanal, ending six months' resistance.

14-16—Rostov and Kharkov seized by Russians.

22—Canadian corvette *Weyburn* strikes mine and sinks near Gibraltar.

Landing in Italy—September 1943

23—Allies halt German drive in central Tunisia.

March

2—Canadian budget introduces unique pay-as-you-go income tax.

2-4—Large portion of Japanese fleet destroyed in Battle of Bismarck Sea near New Guinea.

5—British, Canadian bombers open Battle of Ruhr, begin major year-long offensive against Germany.

28—Eighth Army smashes Germans' Mareth Line in southern Tunisia.

April

7—Eighth Army links up with other Allied troops in Tunisia.

May

12—Organized enemy resistance in Tunisia ends. African campaigns over.

17—With 30 RCAF men in its crew, RAF squadron smashes Ruhr Valley dams.

22—Admiral Dönitz withdraws U-boats from North Atlantic. The crisis is over. The Allies dominate the Atlantic.

30—Americans retake Alaskan island of Attu from Japanese.

June

26—Three-squadron RCAF bomb wing begins operations from North Africa in prelude to invasions of Sicily, Italy.

July

10—Canada's 1st Division, after 3½ years in Britain, invades Sicily with British, American troops.

22—Canadians capture Assoro, Leonforte.

24—Bomber Command launches devastating week-long attacks on Hamburg, Germany, with new device called Window to counter radar defenses.

25—Mussolini resigns as Italy's leader. Marshal Pietro Badoglio takes over.

28—Canadians take Agira.

August

5—Russians take Orel in new offensive.

15—U.S., Canadian forces land on Alaska's Kiska Island, find Japs gone.

17—Sicily conquered. Roosevelt, Churchill confer in Quebec City, plan 1944 landings in France. Canadian, British bombers heavily damage flying-bomb research site at Peenemünde, Germany.

23—Russians retake Kharkov.

September

3—British, Canadian troops land at foot of Italian mainland, strike north.

8—Italy surrenders.

9—British, Americans land at Salerno, Italy.

10—Germans seize Rome. Italian fleet is turned over to Allies.

12—Mussolini freed from detention by German paratroopers.

13—Canada disbands two home-defense divisions.

16—German attempt to wipe out Salerno beachhead collapses.

20—Canadian destroyer *St. Croix* lost to Germans' new acoustic torpedo.

24—In Russia, Germans abandon Smolensk.

ber

-Allies capture Naples.

-Italy declares war on Germany.

-Canadians in Italy take Campobasso and turn it into "Canada Town" recreation center. Disastrous U.S. daylight air raid on Schweinfurt, Germany.

-RCAF sinks fourth U-boat in seven weeks.

-Troops sail from Scotland to raise Canadian forces in Italy to corps strength.

28—Russians gain control of Germans' escape corridor from Crimea.

November

1—Americans invade Bougainville in Solomon Islands.

3—U.S. freighter *Volunteer,* loaded with explosives, catches fire in Halifax harbor. City saved from disaster by courage of navy men.

American dead at Buna in New Guinea—December 1943

6—Russians take Kiev.

18—Bomber Command opens campaign against Berlin.

20—American forces land on Makin and Tarawa in the Gilbert Islands.

25—Eighth Army smashes across Italy's Sangro River.

December

1—At Teheran in Iran, Roosevelt, Churchill, Stalin vow destruction of German forces.

2-3—U.S.-Canadian First Special Service Force takes Mount la Difensa on Italy's Cassino front.

8-9—Canadian troops cross Moro River, open bloody new campaign in Italy.

14—Maj. Paul Triquet wins V.C. in capturing Casa Berardi, north of Moro.

15—Americans win New Britain bridgehead at Arawe in Pacific.

21—Canadians begin savage house-to-house fight in Ortona.

24—U.S. Gen. Dwight Eisenhower named to direct Allied invasion of Europe.

26—Canada announces retirement of General McNaughton as commander of First Canadian Army. German battle cruiser *Scharnhorst* sunk by British off Norway.

27—Germans withdraw from Ortona.

31—RCAF at its peak, with 215,000 men and women, 78 squadrons, including 35 overseas and 6 heading there. Canada has produced 11,000 planes.

1944

January

2—Americans, Australians take Buna in New Guinea.

6—Russians advance into Poland.

14—Canadian secret agent Guy Bieler captured by Gestapo in France.

22—Allies establish Anzio beachhead south of Rome. On Adriatic coast, Canadians man static front.

February

2—Russians enter Estonia and open offensive against Latvia. In Pacific, Americans capture Roi-Namur Island, in Marshalls.

7—Americans take Kwajalein, prewar Japanese territory.

15—Allied bombing, shelling ravage historic Monte Cassino Monastery at key point in Italian battles.

18—Americans attack Truk Island in Pacific.

March

15—Japanese attack India for first time.

20—Russians break into Romania. German troops enter Hungary to counter Russian threat to Balkans.

30—Disastrous raid against Nuremberg ends Bomber Command's 1943-44 offensive against Germany. Planes assigned to support preparations for invasion of France.

April

8—RCAF dive-bombers begin attacks leading up to D-Day.

10—In Crimean offensive, Russians recapture Odessa, long in German hands.

15—Tarnopol, German stronghold in the Ukraine, falls to Russia.

18—British, Indians drive Japanese back in India.

22—Americans land in Hollandia, Netherlands New Guinea.

25-26—Canadian warships sink German destroyer off France.

29—Destroyer *Athabaskan* sunk off France. *Haida* drives flaming German warship aground.

May

4—RCAF says it has destroyed three U-boats in less than a month.

7—Frigate *Valleyfield* torpedoed.

9—Sevastopol naval base recaptured

ALLIES 7 MILES IN FRANCE

by Russians after three-week siege.

11—Allies launch great offensive south of Rome. Canadian tanks in action near Cassino.

18—Cassino, outflanked, is evacuated.

22—Two new RCN motor torpedo boat flotillas begin operations off France.

23—Canadians break through Hitler Line in Italy's Liri Valley.

25—Maj. J. K. Mahony wins V.C. for holding bridgehead over Melfa River.

June

4—Rome, virtually undamaged, falls to Allies.

6—Allies land in Normandy to open campaign in western Europe. D-Day attackers include 30,000 Canadian soldiers, sailors, airmen.

7—Landings reported successful along 60-mile front. Canadian spearhead overrun. Other Canadians first to reach D-Day objectives. Japanese retreat in India

after unsuccessful sieges of Imphal, Kohima.

8—Canadian FO. K. O. Moore's Liberator destroys two subs in 22 minutes.

11—Russians begin new attack on Finland.

13—First German flying bombs strike England, opening 2½-month onslaught. Canadian Sgt. Andrew Mynarski's valor on bombing raid wins posthumous V.C.

15—RCAF fighter wings on move into France. T. C. Douglas wins Saskatchewan election, forms Canada's first CCF government. U.S. Superfortress bombers raid Tokyo. U.S. marines land on Saipan in the Marianas.

19—Carrier-borne U.S. aircraft attack Japanese fleet in Battle of the Philippine Sea. Fourteen Japanese ships sunk off Marianas.

21—Okinawa falls to Americans.

25—Americans storm into Cherbourg, France. Allies building up for next phase in Normandy.

26—Stalin hails great victories in Red Army summer offensive as Vitebsk falls.

28—RCAF fighters destroy 26 planes over France.

Canadians hunt German snipers in St. Lambert-sur-Dives—August 19, 1944

Russian advance—summer, 1944

30—RCAF's 162 Squadron scores four U-boat kills in June, including one by Flt. Lt. David Hornell, V.C., and his crew.

July

4—Canadians take Carpiquet, France.

9—Caen falls to British, Canadians. In Pacific, Americans win Saipan.

14—Five Russian armies in offensives aimed at Warsaw, Berlin.

17—War's largest convoy—167 ships —sails into Atlantic escorted by Canadians who now control all Battle of Atlantic escort forces. It meets no opposition anywhere.

18—Japanese admit loss of Saipan is "great disaster." Tojo cabinet resigns. Canadians gain few miles in attacks beyond Caen. Americans capture St. Lô.

20—Hitler escapes attempt on his life.

21—Americans invade Guam in Pacific.

23—First Canadian Army headquarters becomes operational in France under Lt. Gen. H. D. G. Crerar.

25—Americans break through in Nor-

mandy, begin great drive out of original beachhead. Canadians take heavy casualties south of Caen in helping prepare the way.

August

1—Polish patriots rise against Germans in Warsaw.

2—Russians reach Baltic Sea, cut off Germans in Latvia, Estonia.

8—Americans, having conquered Brittany, veer toward Paris. Canadians launch major offensive south of Caen, break through first German defense line. In Quebec election, Maurice Duplessis returns to power. Corvette *Regina* torpedoed.

10—In Pacific, Americans take Guam.

11—Germans evacuate Florence, Italy, as Eighth Army advances. Canadian tanks in offensive.

15—Allies invade southern France with Canadian landing ships, U.S.-Canadian First Special Service Force among attackers.

18—Canadians take Falaise, France, race to close trap on German Seventh Army.

19—Japanese quit India.

21—Falaise gap closed. German Seventh Army crushed. Maj. David Currie wins V.C. in final fighting. RCAF planes destroy or damage 2600 enemy vehicles in four days. At sea, corvette *Alberni* lost.

22—Canadian-manned aircraft carrier *Nabob* severely damaged by torpedo off Norway.

23—Romania surrenders to Russia, joins Allies.

25—Paris liberated. Allies strike deeper into France.

30-31—In Italy, Canadian troops break through Germans' Gothic Line south of Rimini. Germans' Balkan front collapses.

September

1—Canadians take Dieppe. Russians enter Bucharest, Romanian capital.

3—British liberate Brussels.

4—British take Antwerp. Armistice in Russo-Finnish war.

8—First German V-2 rockets land in London.

10-16—Roosevelt and Churchill confer in Quebec City.

12—Canadians clearing Channel ports in France. Americans advance into Germany near Trier. Soviet patrols into eastern Germany.

13—Canadians capture Coriano Ridge in fierce fighting south of Rimini.

14—Russians reach Czech border. Bomber Command renewing air offensive against Germany.

17—Montgomery launches airborne offensive at Arnhem, Holland, to try to get bridgehead over Rhine and shorten war. Canadians besiege Boulogne, France.

19-20—Canadians in Italy win San Fortunato Ridge as Germans fight desperately to hold them back from Po Valley.

21—Greeks, with 1st Canadian Corps, take Rimini. Drive into Po Valley

beckons but Canadian attacks soon become assaults from one river to another in slow, vicious fighting.

25—Battle of Arnhem ends in disaster Canadian engineers help ferry survivors out. Another winter of war looms.

29—Defense Minister Ralston flies overseas to check on reports of infantry reinforcement shortages.

Churchill, Roosevelt and Stalin at Yalta—February 4, 1945

October

1—Canadians take Calais, winding up campaign to clear Channel ports, overrun flying bomb sites. Russians drive deep into Yugoslavia and lower Hungary.

2—First Canadian Army starts drive to clear Scheldt estuary, open great port of Antwerp to shipping. Americans smash through Germany's Siegfried Line for gain of two miles. Warsaw patriots surrender after heroic two-month-long fight against Germans.

5—British land in Greece. Five RCAF pilots combine to destroy first German jet fighter.

6-7—RCAF's No. 6 Group strikes at Dortmund with record 293 bombers, loses two.

9—Ottawa establishes departments of reconstruction, veterans' affairs, health and welfare, latter to administer new family allowances.

14—No. 6 Group attacks Duisburg twice in 16 hours, with total of 501 bombers. British, Greeks occupy Athens. Defense Minister Ralston, back from Europe, urges overseas conscription.

16—H. D. G. Crerar promoted general, first Canadian of that rank in the field.

20—Americans invade Philippines. Belgrade, Yugoslav capital, captured by Russians and partisans.

21-22—Pte. E. A. "Smoky" Smith wins V.C. in Savio River crossing in Italy.

23-26—Crippling blow dealt Japanese fleet in Battle of Leyte Gulf.

25—Destroyer *Skeena* goes aground in Iceland gale, is total loss.

November

1—Ralston resigns as defense minister. General McNaughton takes over with promise to get enough volunteer reinforcements.

6—Russia renounces neutrality pact with Japan.

7—Roosevelt wins fourth term as U.S. President.

8—First Canadian Army's long, triumphant Scheldt campaign over.

12—RAF sinks German battleship *Tirpitz* off Norway.

22—Army Council tells McNaughton only conscription will provide enough reinforcements, members threaten to resign if he doesn't agree.

23—Mackenzie King switches policy, announces 16,000 conscripts to go overseas.

24—Corvette *Shawinigan* lost in Cabot Strait.

27—Air Minister Power quits cabinet in protest against conscription.

28—First convoy reaches vital port of Antwerp. Eisenhower sees the end of Nazism now that Allies' supply problem is licked.

December

3—Civil war erupts in Greece. In Burma, striking south, Allies take Kalewa. Japanese retreat to Irrawaddy River.

4—Canadians take Ravenna, Italy.

7—Mackenzie King government wins Commons' vote of confidence in wake of conscription measure.

16—Germans launch massive offensive

Marines raise U.S. flag on Iwo Jima's Mount Suribachi—February 23, 1945

through Ardennes Forest on western front. Canadians on alert on static front to north.

17—Germans break into Luxembourg, Belgium, head for Antwerp in what becomes known as Battle of the Bulge.

23—Germans' Ardennes offensive stemmed. Minesweeper *Clayoquot* torpedoed off Halifax.

26—Russians encircle Budapest, Hungary.

29—Canada's Flt. Lt. Dick Audet destroys five planes in ten minutes.

1945

January

1—In its last major offensive, Luftwaffe attacks RCAF, other airfields.

9—Luzon, main island of Philippines, invaded by U.S.

17—Russians take Warsaw.

19—German armies in full retreat on 500-mile eastern front.

20—Provisional Hungarian government signs armistice with Allies.

22—Russians in east Prussia, near Oder River in Silesia. Germans finally routed in Battle of the Bulge.

27—Lithuania in Russian hands.

February

3—Americans enter outskirts of Manila, capital of Philippines.

4—First Canadian Corps gets orders to move from Italy to rejoin First Canadian Army on western front. Roosevelt, Churchill, Stalin confer at Yalta to plan occupation and future of Germany.

8—Anglo-Canadian First Canadian Army begins major attack against Germans west of Rhine, north of Ruhr Valley.

13—Germany's Dresden laid waste by bombers.

19—U.S. marines land on Iwo Jima, island 750 miles from Tokyo.

22—Corvette *Trentonian* torpedoed.

26—Sgt. Aubrey Cosens wins V.C. in Rhine fighting.

March

1—Maj. Frederick Tilston wins V.C. in Germany's Hochwald forest.

4—Allies take Meiktila, key Burmese communications center.

7—Americans seize bridge across Rhine at Remagen. Cologne falls to Allies.

9—U.S. bombers flatten 16 square miles of Tokyo.

10—First Canadian Army completes month-long campaign west of Rhine, forces Germans across river.

17—Minesweeper *Guysborough* torpedoed in Bay of Biscay.

23—Allies cross Rhine north of Ruhr.

24—Canadian airborne troops and RCAF squadrons help reinforce troops across the Rhine. Cpl. Fred Topham wins V.C.

Berlin falls to the Russians—May 2, 1945

26—American troops secure Iwo Jima. In Europe, five Allied armies attacking east of Rhine.

31—Canada's air training program terminated after graduating 131,500 aircrew.

April

1—Americans invade Okinawa, 340 miles south of Japan.

7—Russians enter Vienna.

8—Canadians, in midst of final offensive, capture Zutphen, Holland. Five Canadian divisions, two tank brigades now under General Crerar. Canadian cruiser *Uganda* joins British Pacific Fleet.

12—President Roosevelt dies, succeeded by Harry S Truman.

16—Russians begin push for Berlin on 45-mile front. Canadians capture

Groningen, Holland, after four-day battle. Minesweeper *Esquimalt* torpedoed off Halifax.

17—Canadians clear Apeldoorn, Holland.

21—In Italy, Americans and Poles enter Bologna.

22—Military operations halted on Canadian front in western Holland pending decision on feeding hungry population.

23—First Russian troops enter Berlin.

25—Founding conference of United Nations opens in San Francisco. RCAF's No. 6 Group makes last bombing attack. Americans, Russians meet in Germany.

26—British take Bremen, Germany.

28—Mussolini captured and executed by Italian partisans.

29—Food supplies dropped to starving Dutch as Canadians' front lulls.

30—Hitler commits suicide in Berlin. Russian flag raised on Berlin Reichstag.

May

2—Berlin falls to Russians. Germans surrender in Italy.

3—First Canadian Army takes Oldenburg, Germany. Canadian paratroopers link up with Russians in

Wismar. British retake Rangoon in climax to long, brutal Burmese campaign.

4—In Europe, German forces in north surrender. Canadians cease fire.

7—Germans sign surrender at Reims, France.

8—Official VE-Day. Amid widespread celebrations around world, riots engulf downtown Halifax.

4—Australians, in New Guinea, capture Wewak.

June

5—Allies divide Germany into four zones for occupation.

10—Australians invade Borneo.

11—Mackenzie King's Liberals easily win federal election.

21—U.S. takes Okinawa.

26—Fifty nations sign World Security Charter establishing United Nations.

July

4—Canadian troops arrive in Berlin to share occupation.

5—Labor's Clement Attlee defeats Churchill in British election.

10—Nearly 2000 planes hit Japan in continuing attempt to bomb her into submission.

16—First atomic bomb tested in New Mexico.

17—Truman, Stalin, Churchill meet at Potsdam. British fleet, including Canada's *Uganda,* joins in shelling Japan.

18—Thousands evacuate Halifax as fire, explosives threaten naval magazine.

19—Halifax crisis over.

26—Defeat of Churchill government confirmed in Britain. Attlee replaces Churchill at Potsdam.

August

3—U.S. completes iron ring around Japan.

6—Atomic bomb dropped on Hiroshima, Japan.

8—Russia declares war on Japan, attacks Manchuria.

9—Atomic bomb dropped on Nagasaki, Japan. RCN pilot Robert H. Gray sinks Japanese destroyer but is killed; he is awarded posthumous V.C.

14—Japan surrenders unconditionally. The war is over.

September

2—Japanese sign surrender terms on U.S. battleship in Tokyo Bay.

U.S. atom bomb dropped on Hiroshima, and one victim's watch marks the awful moment of nuclear holocaust—August 6, 1945

Picture Credits

Credits for each two-page spread are listed from left to right and from top to bottom, with additional information as needed.

Cover	Albert Krafczyk
1	Imperial War Museum
2-3	Department of National Defense
4-5	William Pugsley
6-7	U.S. Navy
8	Department of National Defense
26	Department of National Defense
28-29	Imperial War Museum
30-31	Ullstein/Photoreporters
54-55	Keystone
56	Canapress
58-59	Department of National Defense
80-81	National Film Board Collection/Public Archives of Canada/ #WR-680; John Hanson; Canada Wide
82-83	Ullstein/Photoreporters
84-85	Agence de Presse Novosti; Globe and Mail
86-87	Ullstein/Photoreporters (right); Kyodo News Service/Wide World Photos
88-89	Department of National Defense/Whitcombe; UPI/ Bettmann Archives
90-91	Saskatoon Star; Sovfoto (right); Department of National Defense
92-93	Canapress; Associated Press/Wide World Photos
94-95	Black Star (right); Ullstein/ Photoreporters
96	Marcel Côté

Illustrator: Michael J. Middleton